GW01018710

101 Greeting Cards

Also by Melinda Coss

Teddy Knits
Big Softies: 35 Great Designer Knits in Mohair

101 Greeting Cards

(and how to make them)

Melinda Coss

Aurum Press

First published 1993 by Aurum Press Limited, 25 Bedford Avenue,
London WC1B 3AT

A catalogue record for this book is available from the British Library

ISBN 1 85410 259 1

10 9 8 7 6 5 4 3 2 1
1997 1996 1995 1994 1993

Design by Don Macpherson

Printed in Spain by Grafos SA, Barcelona.

Contents

Acknowledgements

This book aroused so much enthusiasm amongst my friends and colleagues that it should really be considered a group effort. Firstly my thanks to Judy Newman for her dried flower pictures, creative pop-ups and others. To Jeanetta Turgel for her printed designs, Karen Lewis for her embroidered Jammy Dodger heart, Isobelle Copus for her decoupage and Debbie Harter for her photocopied heart design. Thanks also to Letts Diaries who supplied the birthday information, Don Macpherson who designed this book, Peter Letts who photographed it, and my publisher and friend, Sheila Murphy, who ensured I stayed sane enough to complete it. I also offer apologies from my dog and four cats for any paw marks that might be misconstrued as part of a design.

Introduction

THE HISTORY OF CARDS

There can be nothing so cheery as opening the post in the morning to find a bright and beautiful greeting card among the usual pile of circulars and bills. Somebody is thinking kindly of you, somebody has remembered, and if the card is handmade, with a special and personal message, it really can make your day.

The tradition of card-sending can be traced back to pre-Christian times when small charms and tokens of good luck were exchanged to celebrate the winter solstice. People celebrated the reawakening of Nature which symbolized the victory of life over death, light over darkness and green pastures over snow and ice. In those magical times it was widely believed that gestures of friendship and kindness would disarm the unfriendly gods, and many traditional seasonal customs stemming from this belief have endured long after their original significance has been forgotten.

In Egypt, scent flasks were discovered within the tombs of the Pharaohs bearing inscriptions relating to flowers which heralded the New Year. Scarabs with hieroglyphs spelling out *au ab nab* (all good luck) were also exchanged at New Year. In Rome, branches of laurel or olive were presented as New Year gifts along with honey, which was superseded by cash, considered by Janus in Caesar's day to be 'even sweeter than honey'.

The Christian celebration of Christmas invested these January feelings of goodwill with new meaning, and while Latin countries such as France, Italy and Spain continued to exchange tokens on January 1st, other Western countries tended to combine Christmas and New Year, presenting tokens of goodwill on or before Christmas Day.

The history of the printed card can be traced back to the early years of European engraving; 15th-century cards were printed from wood-blocks and coloured by hand. Many examples of such cards survive, originating in Germany, Italy and Bavaria. Another forerunner of the Christmas card was the Japanese colour print known as the *surimono*, which conveyed special announcements and messages of congratulations and celebrations.

The tradition of giving cards on St Valentine's day can be traced back to Valentine, a Christian who was said to have been 'beaten by clubs and beheaded, at the time of the great heathen festival of love and purification' (Dyer, *British Popular Customs*). Legend asserts that while in prison Valentine befriended the daughter of Asterius, his jailer, and on the eve of his execution sent her a farewell note signed 'From your Valentine'. Several references to Valentine customs were recorded by the 17th-century diarist Samuel Pepys, and by the late 18th century the making and giving of sentimental and comic Valentines was a firmly established custom.

The making of Christmas and Valentine cards was a traditional pastime in Britain during the Victorian era and many hours were spent creating wonderful compositions in paper, lace and embroidery. The effort invested in these creations demonstrated a sincerity of sentiment that has somehow become lost in the high-tech, busy lifestyles of today. Sadder still is the highly commercial element which has reduced card-sending at Christmas time to an act of guilt, and in some families finding the cash to support this required custom can create real hardship.

There is a huge revival of traditional crafts throughout the world which is not only a positive statement against materialistic values but also represents our new ecological awareness and willingness to recycle those things that we have in the past simply wasted. The making and giving of handmade cards could therefore turn us full circle; once more we can regain the pleasures of giving and receiving with real sincerity and, who knows, in doing so we might 'disarm those unfriendly gods' who continue to cause us such concern.

CREATIVE PERSUASIONS

This book is intended to persuade you that producing your own greeting cards is a pleasurable and valuable pastime. I am not going to give you step-by-step instructions to follow religiously; I am simply going to offer you a bundle of resources that you can tap into, build on and colour in your own way. After all, a card is supposed to convey a personal message and, as a pleasing form of communication, the giving of cards shouldn't be reserved for traditional festivals such as Christmas and birthdays. If you have something you want to say, be it 'I love you' or 'Get lost', the message will have a very powerful significance if it is received in the form of a card which you have obviously spent time and effort in creating. By effort I am not suggesting that you should spend hours slaving over a hot pot of glue; it should simply represent the difference between trotting down to your local card shop and emptying out your wallet and sacrificing an evening's television in the cause of making a card. Most of the cards in this book took less than an hour to make. Those that took longer, such as the patchwork and the crochet, gave me a chance to explore crafts which I normally wouldn't have the time to embark on. 'Patchwork' has always meant 'giant bedspread' to me and 'crochet' either 'jumper' or worse still 'blanket' – projects which I will reserve for later years when I have time to sit for hours in my rocking chair in front of a blazing fire. It has been great fun, therefore, to teach myself the basic principles of these crafts and to have a worthwhile, completed project at the end of the exercise.

There is a wealth of books on the market that will give you a detailed approach to some of the crafts I have used, and you may well discover your own favourite pastime through the making of a card. For the purposes of this book I have taken a novice's approach on the grounds that if an innocent like me can achieve pleasing results with a crochet hook, a pot of silk paint or a lump of dough, then you certainly can too.

THINKING IT THROUGH

Since some of the methods in this book require specific materials, you might find it worthwhile to create a stockpile of cards to cover seasonal events such as Christmas. For example, it isn't worth making up a lump of dough for just one card, so you could begin with a birthday list for all your favourite people and make a baking tray full of items that will suit their individual personalities, thus completing a year's worth of cards at one sitting. For this reason, this book is divided into techniques rather than into card-giving events. The Occasions and Ideas section at the back will give you a number of ideas for images that you could use for particular occasions.

Before beginning, it is very important that you think carefully about the person you are sending the card to – is he a fishing fanatic? what is her favourite flower? etc. If you are going to the trouble of making the card then it should be as personal as possible.

You should also think of your method of delivery; I am not including instructions for making envelopes since I consider this an unnecessary chore when they are so cheap to buy. It might therefore be advisable to purchase an assortment of different-sized envelopes so you can tailor the size of your card accordingly.

I would recommend that dough-craft cards are delivered by hand – unless of course you choose to caption them 'oh crumbs', in which case it won't matter if they arrive in pieces. On the subject of envelopes, you could of course decorate these as well. Sealing wax seals always look very grand and provide the recipient with a moment of suspense. Alternatively you could use a potato cut to print brightly coloured images on the inside (or outside) of the flap, but spare a thought for the postman who has to find the address among all your wonderful design work.

READY-MADE IMAGES

As with many crafts, once you have become hooked on card-making you will never see everyday objects in the same light again. Empty tins of cat food suddenly take on a new life as 'circular templates', old clothes have their buttons removed before they are sent to the jumble, and toffees are bought not for their gooey deliciousness but for their pretty wrappings – excellent for card-making! If you are a cross-stitch fanatic, all those expensive fabric offcuts take on a new lease of life, and flowers no longer find themselves sitting prettily in teapots on your kitchen table but are flattened between the pages of your telephone directory in preparation for your next creative endeavour. Corks, string and even toilet paper all become dual-purpose, and many a fruitful day will be spent combing through other people's castoffs at car boot and garage sales in the search for bits of unusual fabric, beads and lace offcuts.

If you intend to concentrate on papercrafts, magazines are a wonderful source of cutouts for decoupage and general inspiration. If you are not confident about drawing freestyle, keep a file of interesting images that you can trace on to your card.

Printed Christmas cards and wrapping papers are a great resource for the card-maker as images can be recycled in a fresh and interesting way. Keep a notebook to jot down jingles and phrases that could be appropriately re-used, but do avoid anything that might be someone else's copyright, such as Mickey Mouse.

If you do not have an office worker in your immediate circle of friends and relatives it is a good idea to build up a relationship with your local photocopy shop. These magical machines can enlarge, reduce and reproduce images of your choice onto a whole variety of background papers to provide you with outline designs which you can then colour in or enhance with highlight pens. They are also a very cheap method of reproducing family photographs which can be incorporated into Christmas cards for relatives who may have forgotten how much you've all grown.

BASIC MATERIALS

Where necessary, specific equipment for each craft is listed under the various technique headings. However, it is a good idea to set yourself up with some very basic items that will always be useful. While you might be happy working many projects on your lap, you must ensure that you have a good light or all your efforts could produce badly finished cards that you wouldn't send to your worst enemy. I list below various items that you might like to invest in. Because you are sensible readers – if you weren't you wouldn't have bought this book – I know you will take care to keep sharp objects and plastic bags out of the reach of children.

Your most basic material will of course be the card itself. Several clever manufacturers have caught onto the idea of home card-making and are producing blank cards with interesting pre-cut windows (see Stockist Information, p.90). Whether or not you choose to invest in these depends entirely on the amount of time and effort you want to put into your project. Most of the pre-cut cards I have seen are produced in a good choice of colours and finishes and several have standard messages already printed inside. They are excellent for stitchers who wish to concentrate on their stitching and for fabric and doughcraft workers, since they do provide a highly professional finish. The paper-crafters and extremely ecology-conscious among us will undoubtedly prefer to produce their own cards from scratch, so a set of basic templates for tracing is provided at the back of this book for that purpose.

Some wonderful handmade papers are becoming readily available. You could of course go the whole hog and make your own paper, which is a rewarding craft in its own right. See the Recommended Reading list at the back for further information on this subject.

Lay It Out

60cm (2ft) square piece of card or hardboard to work on
30cm (1ft) square piece of card to cut on
Sheets of white and coloured cards and papers
Tracing paper

Measure It

Ruler
Set square
Graph or squared paper
Compass

Cut It

Sharp scissors for fabric
Round-ended scissors for paper
Craft knife or scalpel with extra blades
Hole punch
Pencil sharpener

Stick It

Rubber-based adhesive such as Copydex
Clear adhesive such as UHU
Paper glue-stick such as Pritt Stick
Sellotape

Decorate It

Fine-nibbed black outline pen (the Edding range has a good selection; see Stockists Information, p.90)
Assortment of felt-tipped pens in different colours and thicknesses
Assortment of fancy pens, e.g. gold, silver, glitter, fluorescent, flat-nibbed for italics, etc.
Tippex or other liquid correction fluid
Pencils, crayons, acrylic paints, coloured inks
Eraser

WORKING WITH

Paper

SOURCES FOR PAPER

Paper is a cheap, readily available material that offers a wealth of possibilities to the card maker. Modern packaging material is often more expensive than the item it is designed to protect, so card-making provides the perfect opportunity for recycling. Listed right are papers that should be treasured instead of trashed.

For those who are into begging, borrowing and stealing, fruit and vegetable markets are a good source for coloured tissue papers. If you happen to have a commercial printer near by, they often dump huge bags of offcuts and misprinted showcards – papers which can assist your creativity enormously.

Gold, silver and coloured stars (like those you were given for being especially good at school) are easily purchased from general stationers, as are self-adhesive luminous labels which can be great fun to design around.

Materials

If you have set yourself up with the basic equipment listed on p.3 you will already have everything you need. If you want to achieve some really special effects, there are specialist paper shops selling a wonderful selection of interesting papers from pseudo-snakeskins to holograms (see Stockist Information, p.90).

TREASURE – NOT TRASH!

Cellophane
Corrugated packaging
Cosmetic packaging
Doilies
Gift wrappings
Greaseproof paper (or tracing paper)
Kitchen foil
Lightweight card
Magazines
Paper packaging straw
Paper bouquet ribbons
Seed packets
Sweet and cake wrappings
Tissue paper
Used postcards and greeting cards
Wallpaper offcuts
Metallic cards

A ROSE FOR MY TRUE LOVE
One simple rose cut from a magazine and surrounded with scattered sequins and beads. Use pinhead amounts of clear adhesive to stick down the beads.

DECOUPAGE

Decoupage, the art of cutting and sticking, was popular during the late 17th and 18th centuries and was designed to imitate the freehand painting of highly prized lacquer-ware, imported into Europe from the Far East. Many specialist papers were produced for this simple scissor art, with beautiful cutouts which were glued to the item requiring decorating, hand-coloured and coated with numerous layers of varnish.

Greeting cards provide you with an everyday application for this art and the rich photographic images reproduced in smart magazines offer a wealth of 'cut and stick' material to inspire both traditional arrangements and fresh modern ideas.

CONGRATULATIONS ON THE NEW ARRIVAL
Use a baby cut out from a magazine and surround him or her with cuddly toy cutouts. The frame for this card was drawn freestyle using crayons.

The overall effect of your project will depend entirely on your selection and arrangement of cutouts and these should be chosen to take into account the following points:

First, the recipient: does she/he like flowers, cats, dogs . . . ? Second, the occasion: birthday, get well soon, party invitation, etc. Finally, the colour arrangement: brights, pastels, black and white – you will have most success if you stick to one overall colour story.

When you have selected your images arrange them as a composition on light- or medium-weight card and, when you are happy with the effect, simply fix them down with paper glue – a stick glue is perfect. For added depth and protection the finished card can be varnished but this is not essential.

BUTTERFLY GIRL
This is a lovely card for mum to send to daughter. Cut out a photograph of your daughter and surround her with the things she likes most. Add some sparkly beads or dried flowers and you have a very personalized card.

ALL THAT JAZZ
Fifties jazz cutouts are ideal for a party invitation, and illustrate the different moods and styles you can achieve with decoupage.

CUPPY CAT
This big ginger Tom will be warmly received by any cat lover. You might also consider photocopying a photo of your family pet and surrounding him or her with decoupage cutouts.

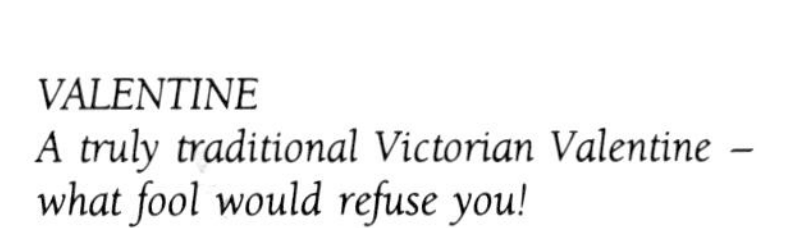

VALENTINE
A truly traditional Victorian Valentine – what fool would refuse you!

CHRISTMAS GIFT WRAP
Re-use last year's Christmas wrapping paper to make this year's Christmas cards. Add a large satin bow and you're there.

DECORATIVE PAPERS

Fancy decorative papers are a great source of inspiration and can be used in numerous ways. They can be salvaged from cake and sweet packaging or purchased in speciality paper shops. Here also is an opportunity to re-use those Christmas and birthday wrapping papers that one never knows quite what to do with. This approach to card-making is perfect for children.

Many papers simply need arranging as a collage. Alternatively they can be scrunched, cut into flower shapes or arranged to give a three-dimensional effect.

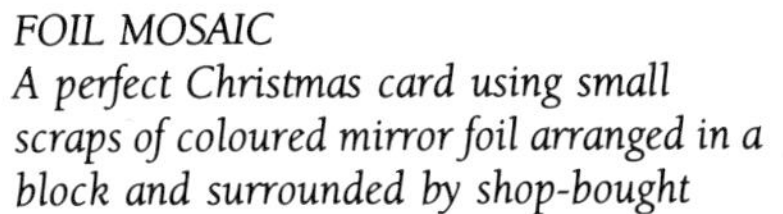

FOIL MOSAIC
A perfect Christmas card using small scraps of coloured mirror foil arranged in a block and surrounded by shop-bought stars. If you can find larger pieces of mirror foil you could stick them on a board and cut them out like a jigsaw.

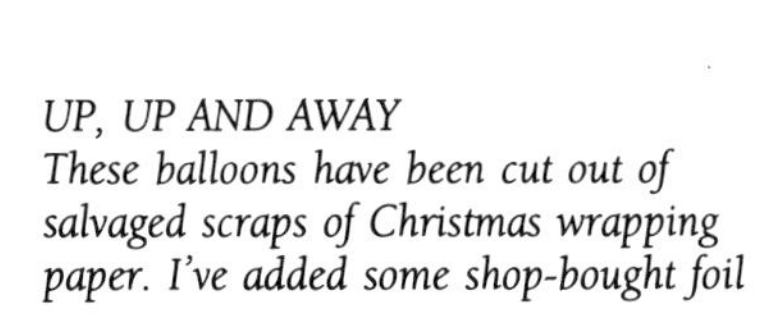

UP, UP AND AWAY
These balloons have been cut out of salvaged scraps of Christmas wrapping paper. I've added some shop-bought foil stars, but if you don't have any, draw in stars with gold and silver felt tips. Perfect for a party invitation.

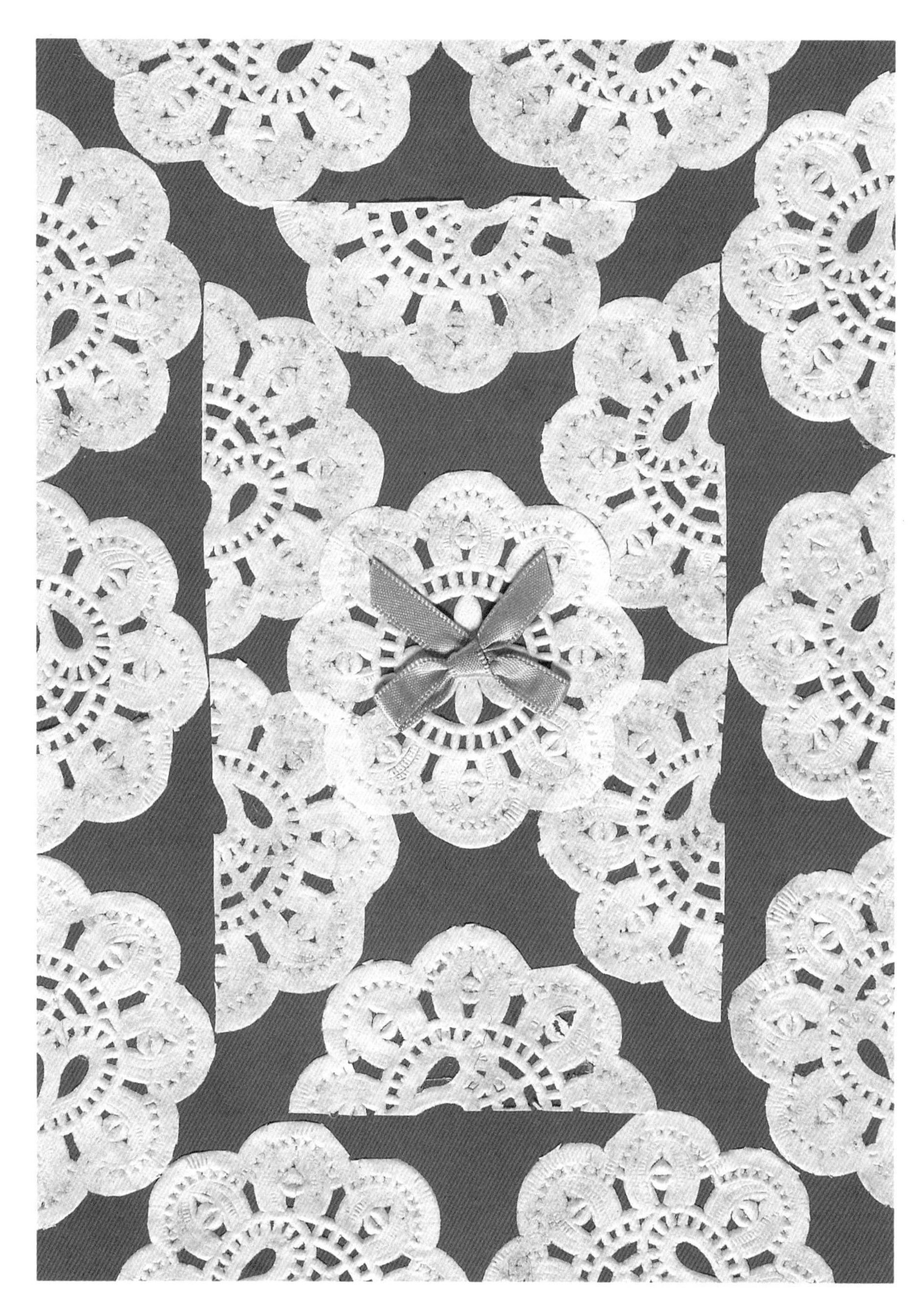

STARRY, STARRY NIGHT
I couldn't resist this hologram paper which I bought at Paperchase in London (see Stockist Information, p.90). Another idea would be to lay foil over a coin and rub it with the side of a ruler to make a raised impression. Glue several foil coins on a card and caption it 'pennies from heaven'. Ideal for a friend who has just got a pay-rise or won the lottery.

ON YOUR WEDDING DAY
This card was made by cutting out the motifs on one paper doily and arranging them in an interesting design on the card. Add a small satin bow and you have the ideal wedding greeting. Doilies can also be cut out to form lacy frames for fabric and decoupage collages.

3-D CARDS

With the use of a few easy techniques and devices, three-dimensional, animated and pop-up images will add great interest to your basic card. In most cases it is a question of clever folding or the positioning of dangly cut-outs.

Since this book is intended to be inspirational rather than fully instructional I have suggested some specialized books on papercrafts and origami (see Recommended Reading, p.90) which will give you far more ideas than I have room to provide. However, the following will explain how I achieved my cards and will hopefully spur you on to greater things.

Rabbit Pop-Up

This illustrates the use of windows, which can be incorporated in lots of ideas including an Advent calendar. To make a window you can take one of two approaches. In this case I have folded a medium-weight card in two and with a pencil and ruler outlined the areas that I wanted to 'open'. With a sharp craft knife I have cut these areas on three sides and run along the fourth edge with the blunt side of a scissor blade to form a fold or hinge. I have drawn the rabbits freestyle directly on to the inside of the card, but if you are not happy drawing you can cut out pictures from a magazine and glue those inside your 'windows'.

The alternative approach is to make your basic card from lightweight card and then cut a second piece of lightweight card exactly the same size as the front. Follow the instructions above for cutting out the windows and, after positioning your images on the front of the original card, glue the sheet with the cut windows directly on top of it.

You can make as many windows as you choose and instead of the felt carrot as a 'window handle' you could use any image appropriate to the message of your card.

Sunflower (p.12)

This pretty sunflower will stand up on its own. Full instructions are given below. Templates on p.82.

Materials

1 sheet each A4-sized heavyweight paper in green, yellow and tan
1 pearl
11 long green sequins
11 long gold sequins
42 long turquoise sequins

N.B. You don't have to use sequins – as an alternative, paint pieces of spaghetti in whatever colours you wish and cut them into half-centimetre lengths.

Instructions

1. Fold the A4 piece of green paper in half and by laying the base template against the fold, cut out a double image as shown.

HOPPY BIRTHDAY
Open the hatches and watch the rabbits multiply. You can use this window technique for an Advent calendar.

Instructions for Sunflower (contd.)

2. Trace the Sunflower template on to the yellow and tan paper and cut one of each.

3. Glue the yellow flower-head on top of the tan flower-head, positioning the petals alternately as shown on the photograph.

4. Glue the flower-head on to the base, lining up the petals.

5. Cut a circle of tan paper for the centre of the flower and glue down.

Decorate centre with pearl and beads as shown on photograph.

GET WELL SOON
This sunny sunflower would brighten any sick-room, and it doesn't need watering.

Mr Crab

This smart fellow, wearing a wrapping paper waistcoat, is designed to hold a placecard at the dinner table. This is how he was made (templates on p.83):

Materials

1 sheet each of heavyweight paper in red, black and white
Oddment of gift wrapping paper
2 split peas
Black felt-tipped pen
Paper glue-stick

'Mr Crab' will hold a placecard between his claws so your dinner guests know exactly where they are supposed to sit.

Instructions for Mr Crab

1. Trace base template on to red paper and cut one. Fold sides in to centre, along dotted lines.

2. Trace waistcoat section on to wrapping paper and cut one. Glue into position on base.

3. Trace and cut out shirt top and bottom pieces in white paper. Glue into position.

4. Trace and cut out bow tie in black paper and glue on to shirt top where indicated with an x.

5. Trace and cut out two claws in red paper, one reversed.

6. Trace and cut out two sleeves in black paper, one reversed. Glue into position on top of claws. Carefully cut two slits in claws as indicated by dotted line.

7. Trace and cut out left and right jacket backs in black paper; glue into position on back of main body.

8. Glue claws into position as indicated on template.

9. Draw in mouth and stick on two split peas for eyes as shown.

10. Cut a piece of white paper approximately 12cm ($4^3/_4$in) long and 2.5cm (1in) wide for namecard and slot into claws.

One Today

This little boat bobs across the waves and is simple to make. Templates on p.84.

Materials

1 A4 sheet of red card for background
Small sheets of blue and green card, or one sheet of white card if you prefer
Paper glue-stick
Red, yellow and brown felt-tipped pens

Instructions

1. Fold your base card in half and cut two slits across the front approximately 4.5cm ($1^3/_4$in) up from the bottom and 10cm (4in) wide, leaving 1cm (½in) in between.

2. Your wave template gives the size for the bottom wave. You need to cut seven waves (four blue and three green) slightly lengthening the depth at the bottom of each one as you go. Glue two of these on to the main card approximately 1cm above your cuts as indicated on the photograph.

3. Stick the remaining waves on top of each other and glue to the card at the edges only.

4. Trace boat template (including 'stick') and cut this out of white paper.

5. Colour in bottom of boat in red and sail in yellow with joining 'stick' in brown.

6. With white paper cut another stick shape to end at the dotted line as indicated on template. Glue the top of this into position on the back of the boat.

ONE TODAY
This cheerful little birthday boat bobs along on the blue sea.

One Today (contd.)

7. Slot the bottom stick through the loose piece of red background card and glue the bottom of the two sticks together leaving the middle area free to slide up and down.

8. Cut a circle out of white paper and colour in with yellow. Position and glue for sun.

CAT WITH NINE LIVES
This cat moves his eyes around and you can colour him in to look like someone's special cat.

Cat With Nine Lives

This cat should be coloured in to match your own favourite feline. The following shows the mechanics of fitting the googly eyes which move from side to side and up and down. Templates on p.85.

Materials

1½ A4 sheets of white card
Paper glue-stick
Felt-tipped pens (green plus cat colours)
Green glitter (optional)
Craft knife

Instructions

1. Fold white card in half with fold at side. Trace cat shape and cut through back and front, leaving areas indicated with dotted line uncut.

2. Cut holes in front half of card for eyes, colour in cat as required.

3. On separate piece of white card, trace and cut out 'flag' marked 'eye template' and draw in eyes, colouring shaded areas in green felt-tipped pen and centres in black. Add glitter to green areas if required.

4. Cut two narrow strips of white card approximately 5cm (2in) long and glue these top and bottom only to the back of the cat image as positioned on template. Slot in the eye flag.

Wise Old Owl

Pull the string and this owl flaps his wings. Templates on p.85.

Materials

1 A4 sheet of lightweight yellow card
½ sheet each yellow, green and orange lightweight card, or colours of your choice
2 paper-fasteners
Paper glue-stick
Paper scissors
Skewer
2 x 20cm (8in) lengths of lurex cord or wool
2 beads (optional)

Instructions

1. Fold card in two. Trace and cut out main template, then lay against fold of card and cut out front and back leaving fold area uncut.

2. Trace and cut out head template in yellow paper and glue into position on front of card. Cut out contrasting nose, eyes and ear centres and glue them into position.

3. With skewer make hole in position marked x.

4. Cut out and glue tummy feathers in overlapping colours on to tummy and trim edges to base shape. With skewer make two holes through tummy in positions marked 1.

WISE OLD OWL
This wise old owl is the perfect card for Dad or Grandpa.

Wise Old Owl (contd.)

5. Trace and cut out two wings and forty wing feathers.

6. With skewer make a hole at top of both wings in position marked 2. Tie one end of lurex through the hole and secure. Repeat for other wing.

7. Push paper-fasteners through wings at position marked 3. Glue wing feathers in overlapping pattern on to wings and trim edges to shape.

8. Push free end of paper fasteners through body holes (position marked 1) and bend back to secure.

9. Thread two free ends of lurex through mouth, thread beads on the end and secure with a knot.

KEEP SMILING SUNSHINE
Cheer a friend up with a smile. A simple approach to pop-ups.

Keep Smiling Sunshine

This card illustrates a very simple way of creating a pop-up effect. I have cut my own basic card from a heavyweight white textured paper and outlined the 'window' with a gold felt-tipped pen. Templates on p.84.

Materials

½ sheet each gold, silver and white card
Blue and orange paper
Paper glue-stick
Piece of white shirring elastic

Instructions

1. Working with a card that measures 29.5cm (11½ in) in width (when open) x 21cm (8¼ in) in height, cut a front window with a top, left and right margin of 2.5cm (1 in) and a bottom margin of 6cm (2¼ in). Cut a strip of blue paper waves (using template as a guide) to fit right across the bottom of your open card.

2. Make three folds in this strip of waves, the first 10.5cm (4in) from the left edge (as you look down at it), folding the left side towards the right side. Measure another 9cm (3½in) along and make a fold going the other way and a further 5.5cm (2in) for the last fold (in towards the centre).

3. Stick both ends down leaving areas between first and third folds free.

4. Cut a second, full-width strip of narrower waves and glue this down flat above the first strip and visible across the bottom of the window opening.

5. Cut four cloud shapes (free-style) and glue these down on the inside of the card, visible through the window opening.

6. Fold a piece of white card in half and, placing the cloud template against the fold, cut a fifth cloud.

7. Make folds 2.5cm (1in) in from both edges and glue these down flat either side of the main fold of the card, adjusting the position so that this cloud lays flat when the card is closed and pops up when it is open.

8. Cut a sun shape from gold card and add to the centre a circular disc of orange paper on which you should draw two eyes and a smiley mouth.

9. Make a small hole and thread a piece of elastic through an arm of the sun and tie it around the folded cloud.

10. Adjust the length of the elastic so that the sun bobs between the clouds and is clearly visible through the window.

POP-UP REINDEER
The card below reveals a pop-up reindeer (see overleaf). I have cut a card from a sheet which is gold on one side and white on the other, but you can use anything you like for a background. Templates on p.84.

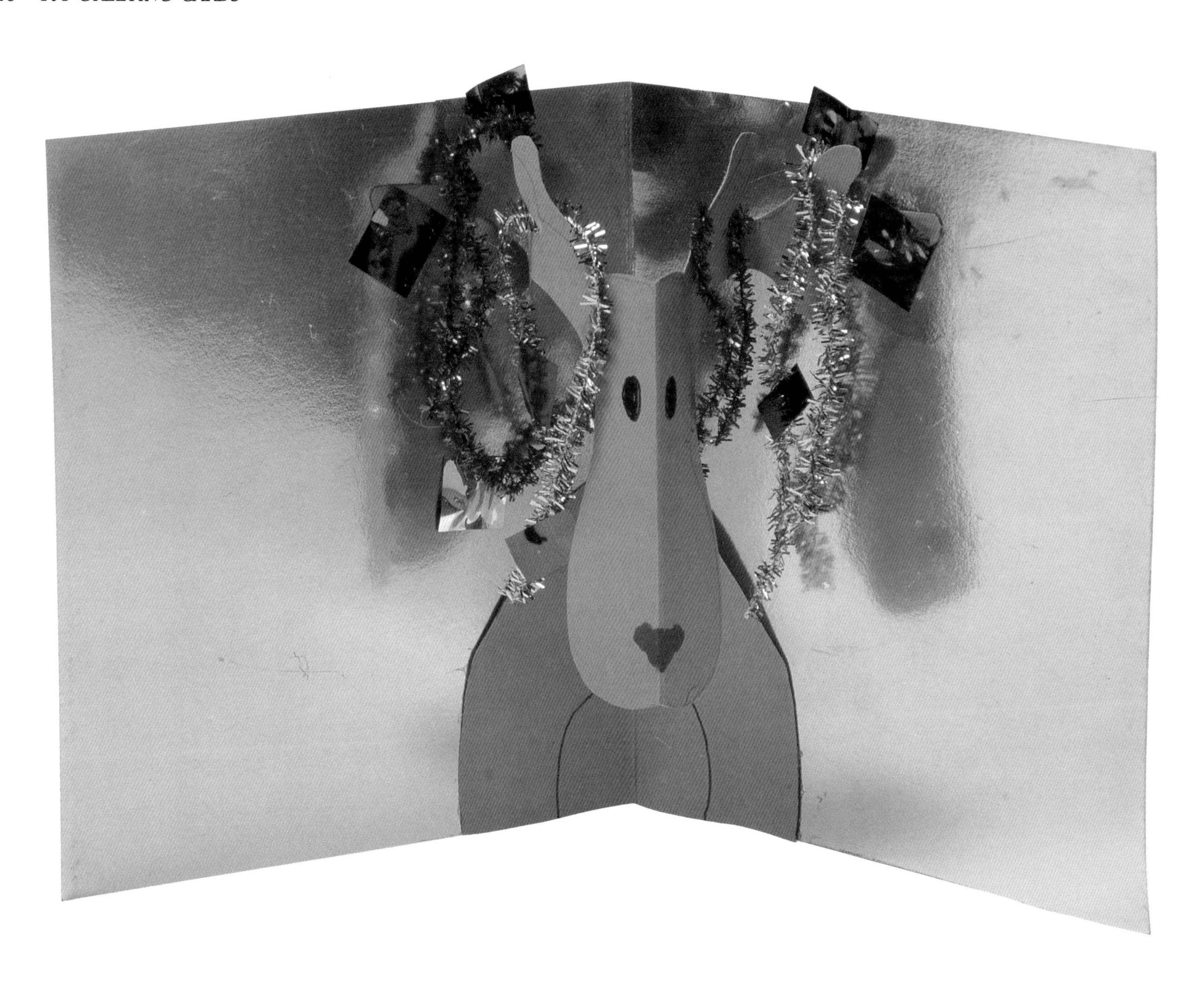

Materials

Lightweight card: brown for reindeer, contrast colour for front
Scraps of foil and tinsel
Black, red and gold felt-tipped pens
Glitter
Clear adhesive

Instructions

1. Write your message on the front of the card with gold felt-tipped pen and decorate with glitter.
2. Fold brown card in half. Trace shape from template and, laying this on the fold of the card, cut out a double image.
3. Fold back the two extreme ends of the antlers and glue these either side of the inside fold of your card, positioning the head so that it lays flat when the card is shut and pops up when open. Draw eyes and nose in position and decorate antlers with tinsel and foil shapes.
4. From remaining brown card cut the body shape, placing this against the fold as indicated on the template. Open this up and draw a smaller half-oval across the centre to indicate a division for the reindeer's front legs. Glue this down flat at the centre bottom of your open card, laying fold over fold.

POP-UP REINDEER
Rudolph dressed in festive gear is sure to bring some Christmas cheer!

SHAPE UP

All sorts of interesting effects can be produced by cutting your card into lifelike shapes and decorating the image. Anyone who went to nursery school must recall cutting strings of paper dolls out of folded newspaper. The same principle can be applied to cards.

Fold your card in two or three and trace and cut out the shape of your choice to create a double or treble image. The only thing you have to remember is to take care not to cut right through your folded edge since this holds the card together. First practise on old news-

HAVING A WHALE OF A TIME
A great bon voyage card. Draw a simple whale shape and cut it double with the fold of the card against the tail. Trim down the front whale so he becomes just a baby and add the water spouts. These whales have been covered with kitchen foil and the baby has been rubbed over with a blue wax crayon.

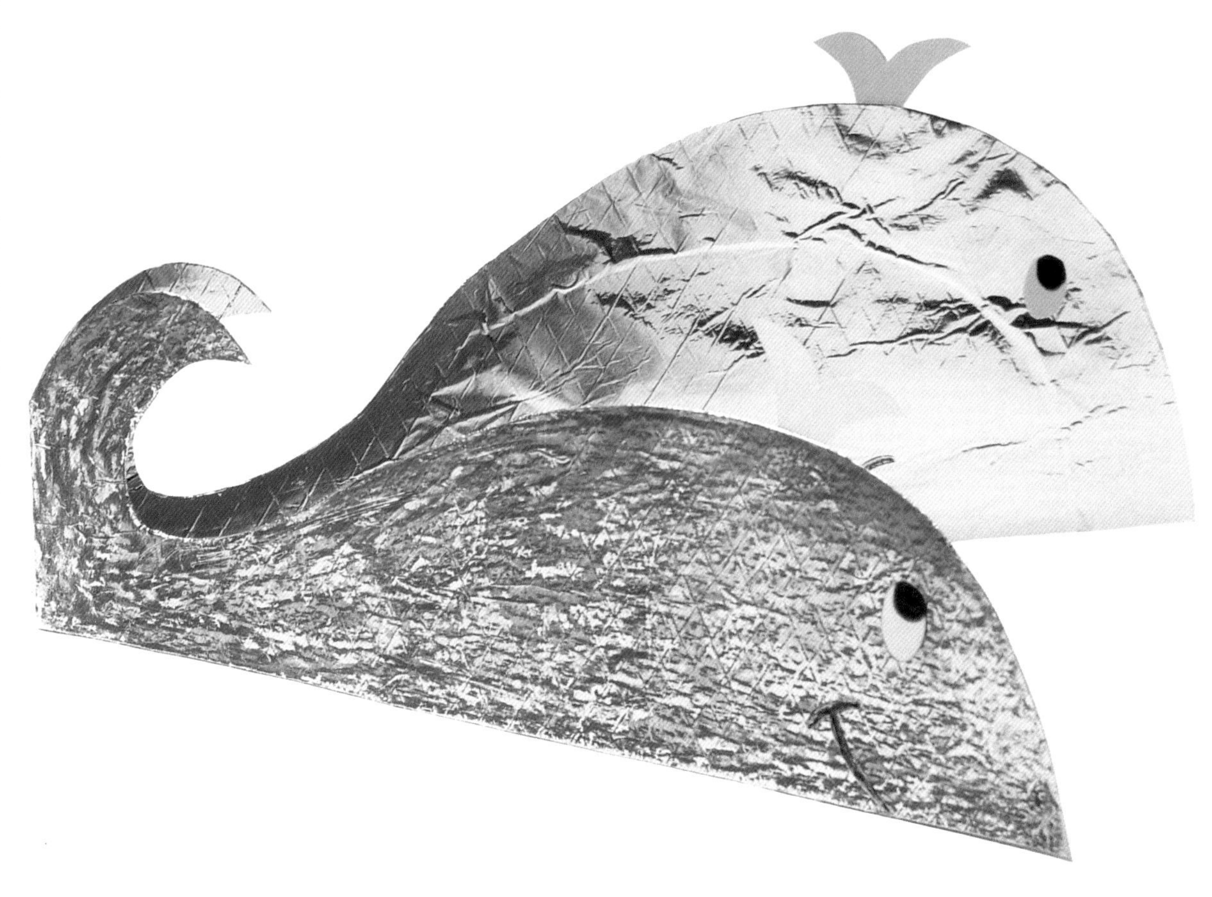

papers, and experiment by folding the paper in various ways and drawing different shapes.

You can customize your card by choosing a particular shape. For example, if you want to send a card to someone who has just moved house, cut out a simple house shape or, using the 'paper doll' technique, a row of terraced houses or a horizon of skyscrapers. I have used a wedding cake for a wedding card but a bell shape in gold or silver card would be equally attractive. Or what about cutting out a pram shape for a new baby?

When you have a shape that you are happy with you can enhance the design by decorating it with luminous felt-tipped or metallic pens or by covering your card with textured paper or foil. You can then add buttons and bows or oddments of beads to complete the composition.

If you are not confident that you can draw your shape freestyle, trace an image from a magazine and have it enlarged at your local photocopy shop. If you trace it on to squared paper, you can enlarge it yourself by drawing your own grid with larger squares than the original and then copying your image square for square. The possibilities are endless.

YOU SNEAKY SO AND SO
A card to celebrate a discovery – an engagement, an examination pass. This is a simple cutout (template on p.86) that has been coloured in with fluorescent pens.

FIERY DRAGON
A dragon's head cut out of red card (template on p.87) and decorated with gold, black and red felt-tipped pens. Add a gold card tongue and you have the ideal card to send for Chinese New Year.

SILENT NIGHT
These little dangly stars have been cut from fluorescent papers laid back to back and stuck together. They are then suspended from the frame of a black card with cotton. Very easy – very effective.

A PIECE OF CAKE
Wedding celebrations are great fun with this card, cut in a very straightforward tiered shape (template on p.86) and decorated with screwed-up pieces of toilet tissue or crepe paper. Old cake decorations have been saved and recycled for the occasion. Alternatively, the cake shape could be decorated with 'something borrowed, something blue . . .'

STENCILLING

Stencilling on both paper and fabric is a traditional technique which is experiencing a resurgence of interest among interior designers.

As a result, numerous ready-cut stencils are available in the shops and books of ready-to-cut stencils can be obtained from bookshops or through libraries. Simple animal and alphabet stencils are also available at stationery shops as stencilling has always been a popular pastime for

STILL SWANNING AROUND
A birthday card for the not-so-young. The swan is cut out of white paper from a commercial stencil and the bulrushes and water are cut from coloured paper and stuck on top of the black shiny card. Several of the green leaves and the front bulrush have been attached to the card only at the bottom to give an extra dimension to the image.

PROUD AS A PEACOCK
This is the perfect card to send to someone you want to congratulate. The tail of the peacock is cut out of your main card and backed with paper in a contrasting colour; the body and feathers are in relief, having been cut from separate sheets of paper and stuck on afterwards. Some bugle beads add a little glitter to the occasion.

HOW DOES YOUR GARDEN GROW?
A 'how are you?' or 'get well' card. Very straightforward flower shapes cut from coloured paper and glued on to your base card. Add some beads for flower centres and your card is complete. A good project for children.

COME TO A PARTY.
You will get the full effect of this stained-glass technique by holding your completed card up to the light. The cutouts are backed with coloured tissue paper. Add a label and cork of silver foil and some shredded tissue streamers.

children. Images can of course be traced and cut out of medium-weight card or acetate by anyone who is confident with a sharp craft knife. Stencilling is also a useful method of producing 'writing' for the inside of your card as plastic rulers and sheets of cut-out letters and numbers are readily available from art and craft shops. (Specialist brushes and paints can also be purchased, but these are not really necessary for card-making purposes.)

Stencilling is a particularly useful technique for when you wish to duplicate your design. Once cut, you can use the cut-out shape as a raised image by sticking it on card (see the swan and paper cut-out flower cards). You can glue different coloured tissue or cellophanes across the back of the cut-out holes to obtain a 'stained glass' effect. Or you can use both the cut-out and relief areas as part of one design, as shown on the peacock. In addition, once you have a cut stencil, you can achieve some delicate shaded effects by sponging, crayoning or spraying colours through the holes either directly on to card or on to fabric which can then be mounted on card.

SPRING BOUQUET
A pretty arrangement for Mother's Day, once again using the stained-glass technique.

WORKING WITH Fabric

If you have a ragbag, a bin liner full of castoffs that you keep meaning to take to the jumble, or if you are simply a hoarder of unfinished curtains, skirts, quilts etc., this is the section for you.

Not only does card-making put your bits and pieces to excellent use, it also gives you the perfect opportunity to try out in a small way traditional skills such as patchwork (which always looks as if it would take a lifetime). You can play with tweeds and velvets and voiles without the headache of having to get seams straight and you can mix and match them with papers and bits and bobs to create wonderful textured collages and room-sets.

Materials

Nearly all the materials you will require are on the basic list on p.3. In addition, a plait of coloured cottons and some sharp sewing needles and pins will be necessary for quilting and appliqué, and a knitting needle and cork tile (for pinning on) will make life easier if you want to try ribboncraft.

COLLAGE

This is the easiest way to use fabric as it requires little more than a good eye for colour. Keep a pinboard full of your favourite postcards and tear out sheets from magazines that you feel could provide you with future inspiration. Colour is used so imaginatively by both nature and the media that it is really just a question of keeping your eyes open and noticing what is going on around you.

Collages can be designed to imitate landscapes or room-sets, to illustrate a fantasy or to present an abstract composition of texture and colour. When making cards you should stick to light- and medium-weight fabrics, as heavy wool can look very clumsy unless used just as a highlight.

ROOM WITH A VIEW
Ideal for a 'new home' greeting, the fabrics in this card have been selected for their likeness to 'the real thing'–the curtaining imitates real net curtaining and the chair covering is a tiny print, a scaled-down version of a typical furnishing fabric. You could produce a bedroom scene as a get-well card and incorporate a mini-sized patchwork quilt. A template for the four-paned window can be found on p.88.

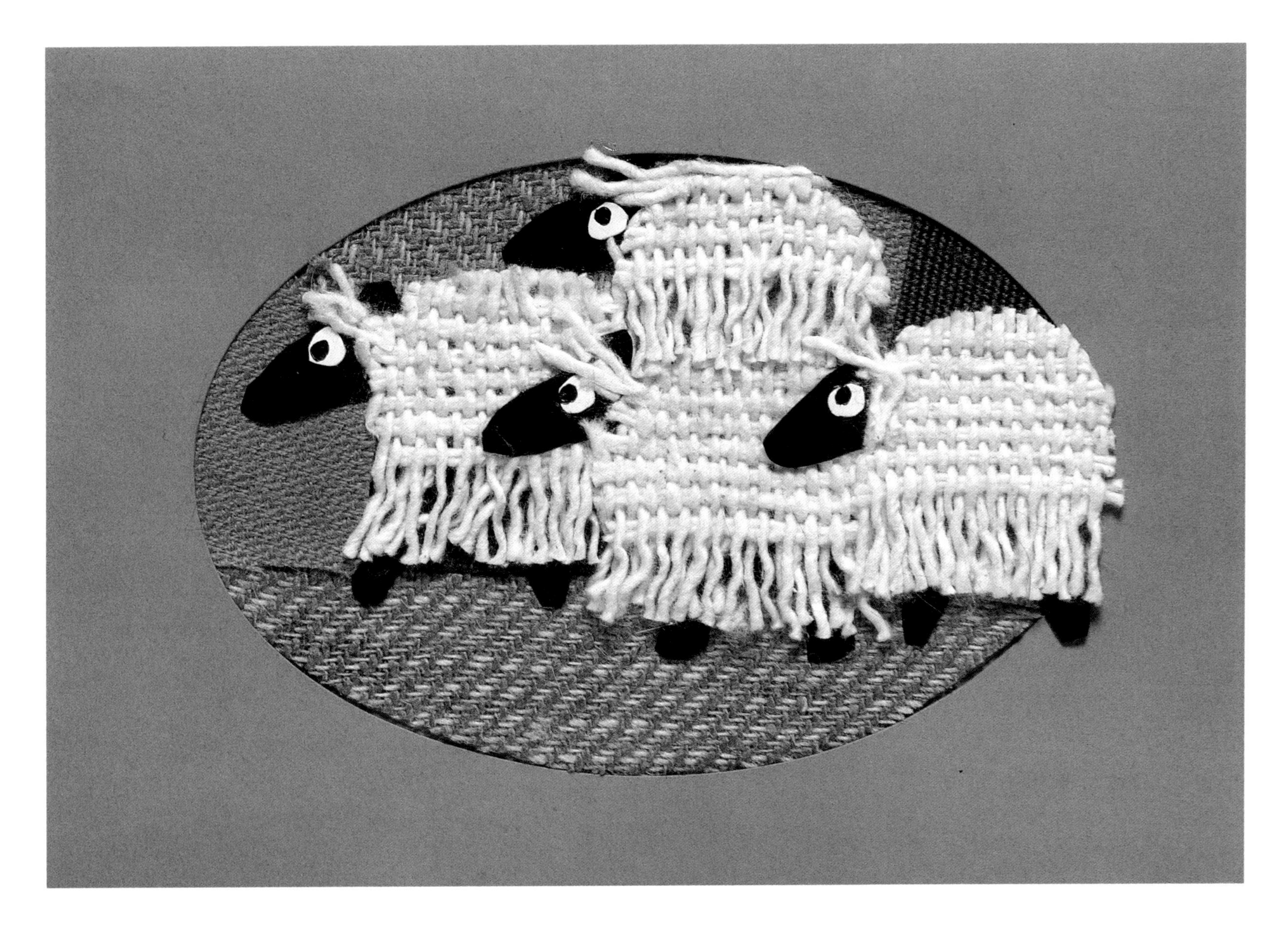

FROM ONE OF THE GANG
The patchwork of meadows consists of glued-on squares of an assortment of lightweight tweed wool fabrics. The sheep themselves are produced from a loosely woven wool and the faces and feet are cut from black card. The white card eyes were glued on once the heads were in position and the black felt-tipped pupils were added to complete the picture. You could use green background fabrics to create a spring landscape.

SEASON'S GREETINGS
This simple Christmas tree card is made by cutting shapes from wide floristry ribbons which can be bought in a wonderful variety of textures and widths (see Stockist Information, p.90). If you don't have access to these, cut a tree shape from card and use plain white netting over the top. For the snow effect you could glue on tiny balls of cotton wool or even silver or white sequins.

ON YOUR RETIREMENT
This card was produced by cutting an oblong of ticking and glueing it top and bottom over two cocktail sticks with their ends trimmed off. The word 'Café' is written freestyle with a black indelible pen and the small pull cord is a length of knotted embroidery cotton glued centre back. The top cocktail stick has then been glued across the top of the window with the bottom left hanging free. You could glue a picture behind the blind or work this idea over a four-paned window cutout (see p.88). If you are sending this to someone extra special, add a window box full of flowers by either drawing one in or cutting one from pieces of coloured card and glueing it into position.

NAUGHTY BUT NICE
Oddments of floral lace and chintz have been carefully cut out and stuck on randomly. Add a couple of satin bows and you have a very pretty collage.

FOR A SWEET HEART
This card has been padded by glueing a thin layer of wadding on to the card before carefully covering it with floral fabric. A heart cut from the same floral fabric has been stuck to the inside of the card and a small bag of lace, filled with lavender, is suspended in the centre by a short length of ribbon.

HAPPY ANNIVERSARY
These two geese are obviously very much in love. Trace the main template on to white felt and cut out two thicknesses. Do the same with the wings and cut the feet and beaks from red felt. Cut two black felt eyes and glue the shapes into position on a green background. Add lurex bows and glue lace trimming around the edge of the card.

CHRISTMAS EVE
For a very quick card-making solution, select a fabric of your choice and glue it inside your card. Highlight areas with a gold or silver felt-tipped pen and add a star or what you will. I have used a bold abstract Liberty print for this design.

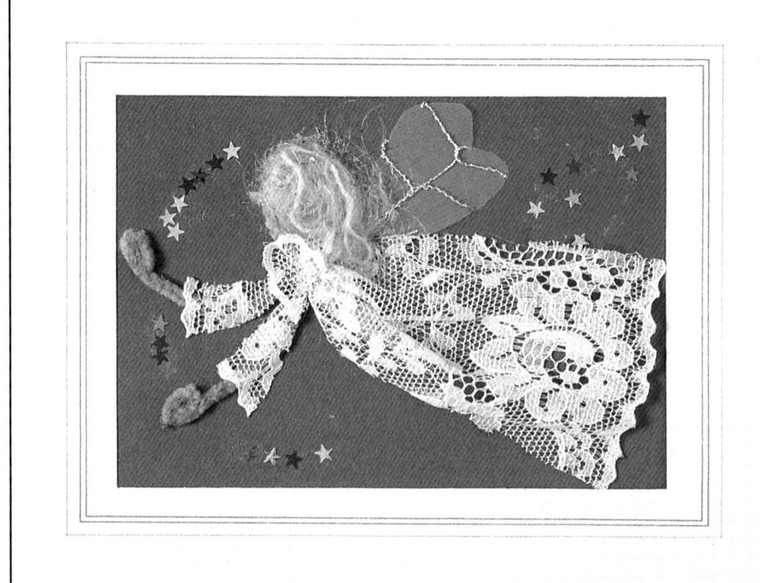

YOU ANGEL!
You will need small offcuts of lace and voile (or net), two pink pipe cleaners, scraps of silver thread and yellow mohair and a scattering of foil stars to produce this angelic card. Bend one pipe cleaner in half and roll the ends for hands; glue into place. Roll the second pipe cleaner to make the angel's face and glue into position. Add some scrunched-up mohair for her hair. Gather an oblong of lace a centimetre from the top to form a collar for her dress and cut out two triangular sleeves to cover her arms. Glue these over the pipe cleaners. Cut a wing shape out of voile and stitch on veins of silver thread. Add a scattering of stars. Use a clear glue throughout.

HAPPY ENDINGS
Silhouettes are made by tracing outlines of images and cutting them out of black paper or fabric. The basic design for this card was traced from an old book and the fabric has been stuck to the outside of the card to form curtains.

RIBBONCRAFT

Ribboncraft is a pleasing and therapeutic pastime which has become an art in its own right. There are now so many varieties of ribbon on the market – from dots and tartans to pictorial prints and glittering lurexes – that the card-maker cannot fail to be inspired. You are bound to come up with numerous ideas and there are various simple techniques to help you realize them.

Weaving

This is probably the simplest and most appropriate technique for card-making since it produces a flat professional finish and can be varied according to the ribbons you select and the shape of your card window. You can choose reds, greens and golds for Christmas, tartans for New Year and pretty pastels for new babies and weddings. Play around by interweaving different thicknesses and finishes of ribbon, and mix and match spots and stripes with plain colours to achieve a patchwork effect. You can buy complete kits designed for card-making (see Stockist Information, p.90).

Materials

Assorted ribbons in various widths
Lightweight iron-on interfacing (optional)
Dressmaker's pins
Cork tile for pinning on
Sharp scissors
Safety pin

Ribbon Weaving

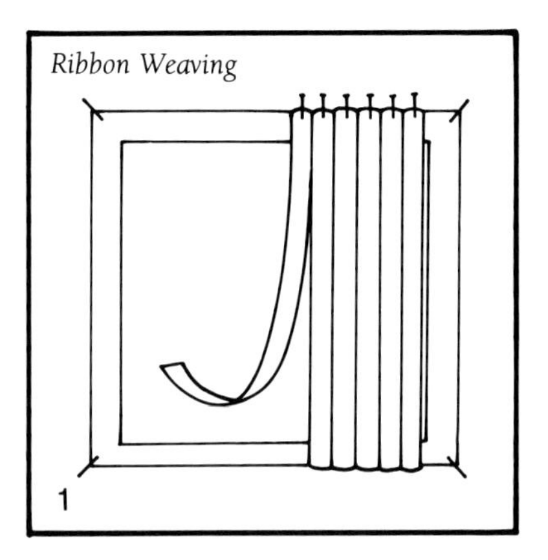

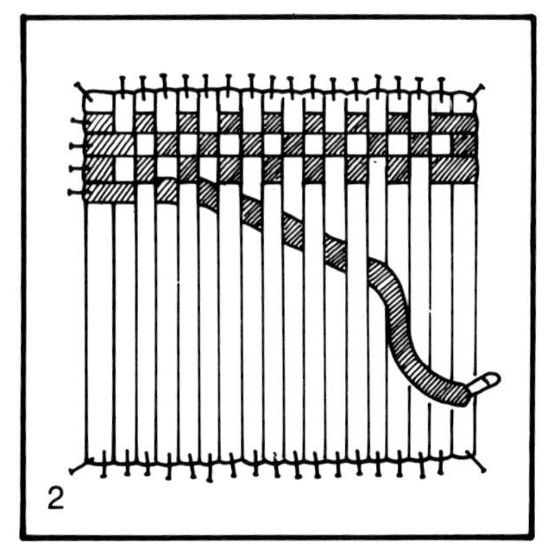

To make a square woven panel follow these basic instructions:

1. Cut a piece of interfacing slightly larger than your finished requirement and lay this on the cork tile, adhesive side up.

2. Cut equal lengths of ribbon. The number of lengths needed will be dictated by the width of the ribbon you select.

3. Pin half of the lengths in a row, touching each other, to form a warp (fig. 1).

4. Using a safety pin as a guide, weave in the weft ribbons and pin ends into position (fig. 2).

5. Iron the work lightly to bond the ribbons to the interfacing.

6. Remove pins and iron the wrong side to bond thoroughly.

7. Cut to shape and glue the panel inside your card.

MY HEART IS IN RIBBONS
Use the simple weaving technique for this card, shading your ribbons through pink, peach and lilac. Mount them on a card with a heart-shaped window. A template is provided on p.88.

Ribbon Embroidery

Narrow ribbons can also be used in the same way as thread for embroidery. Flower petals can be achieved by working in a lazy daisy stitch, catching the ribbons at the centre (fig. 3) and stems can be created by securing with small ribbon stitches as illustrated. I have used simple knots to make the fabric look like rosebuds but a more realistic rose can be made by curling the ribbon and securing it with wire at the bottom. You can then add petals by folding the ribbon back on itself as you wind it around the centre bud.

Ribbons are also formed into rosettes in my New Year card. Cut a length of ribbon and fold it in half lengthwise. Sew a thread in a running stitch along the bottom edge and gather, securing firmly. Stitch the loose ends together to form a circle. You can make a number of these in different widths of ribbon and stitch them on top of each other. What about blue, white and red for Bastille Day?

It is always useful to include narrow ribbons in your basic materials; they can be used as contrasting borders for designs and are excellent for covering up raw edges, especially on fabric collages. If you can't be bothered to make your own, small ready-made bows and rosebuds can be purchased very cheaply and make a charming addition to many designs. Ribbons can also be woven through lace to create a professional finish or cut and glued in strips to create a no-sew patchwork effect.

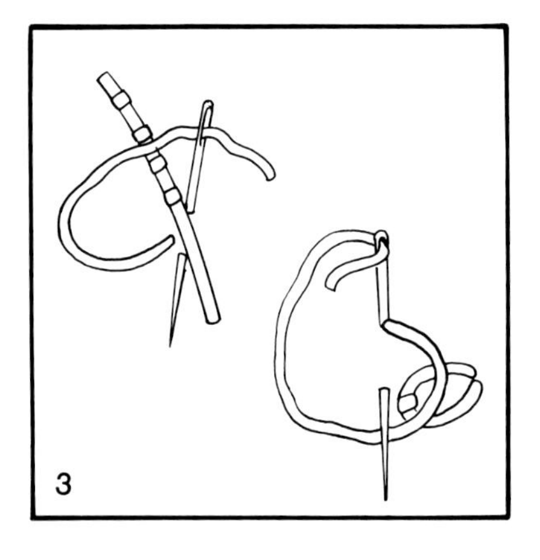

Ribbon Embroidery

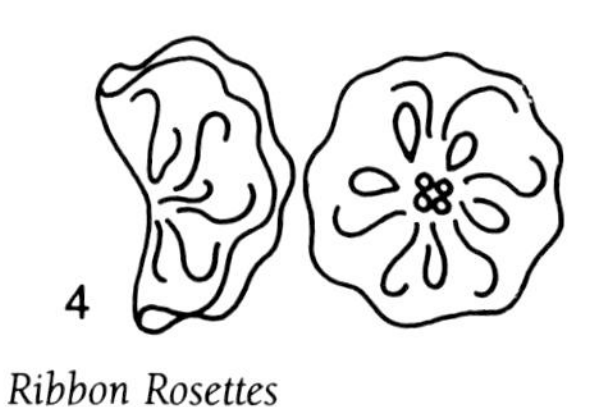

Ribbon Rosettes

VALENTINE
Padded cards are extraordinarily expensive and you can make your own by glueing a square of wadding on to a medium-weight piece of card and covering it with silky fabric. Alternatively, you could cover the card with ready-quilted satin or velvet (the type they sell for dressing gowns and evening wear) then mount a white cotton heart as I have, edged with lace and embroidered with ribbon flowers. Or you can add whatever you choose, making use of rhinestones, pearls, beads and lace trimmings.

CHECKMATE
This card illustrates the cheat's approach to patchwork. Its success depends on your selection of ribbons which are cut into lengths and glued directly on to the card.

SILVER WEDDING CELEBRATIONS
Shades of blue interlaced with a silver-edged ribbon are woven together and mounted behind a circular window. For an extra special card you could add some silver bells or beads from your cake decorating box.

HAPPY NEW YEAR
An arrangement of tartan ribbon rosettes trimmed with leaves cut from a wide green satin ribbon. Glue on to a calico background which has been mounted behind a square frame. Add a pearl and celebrate Hogmanay.

QUILTING, PATCHWORK AND APPLIQUÉ

Quilting is a much-loved pastime often embarked upon to produce a family heirloom which will be passed down from generation to generation. It is a technique I have always wanted to try but, as a textile designer, an occupation which I never felt I could justify because of the time needed to complete a quilt.

There are numerous pattern books on the market and as many variations of design and shape as there are stitches in a knitting technique book. If, like me, you would like to experiment with this skill, card-making provides you with the perfect opportunity to try it out in miniature.

The secret, as with most design projects, is the selection of colours and patterns, although you can often surprise yourself by producing combinations that look stunning but would not work in any other medium. It depends on the choice of shapes which tone down the stronger patterns or highlight the weaker ones, or the redistribution of the weight of a design by the simple method of mixing plains with heavily patterned florals.

While a multi-coloured mish-mash seems to work fine, take special care in the selection of fabric weights. Don't mix heavy tweeds with lightweight cottons or you will end up with a lumpy conglomeration that will not be fit to send to anyone worthy of receiving your card.

The above refers only to the

GET WELL SOON
My little hexagonal patchwork quilt is sewn from a number of small print fabrics and I intended to incorporate a mouse underneath it wearing a nightcap with a tassel. Since I couldn't find a mouse who would stay still long enough to be photographed, you will have to do without one.

THE ROAD TO TRUE LOVE NEVER RAN SMOOTHLY
Cheer up a lovelorn soul with this little patchwork, produced from a variety of fabrics cut into one single width and stitched in a never-ending path.

STAR TURN
This design presents you with an optical illusion. It could be a large central star, tumbling blocks or a zigzag road, depending which way you look at it.

traditional patchwork quilts of North America. The Welsh are also famous for their quilts but their workmanship is concentrated on the use of plain rows of stitching sewn in intricate patterns through three layers of fabric.

To make a patchwork design you will require the following:

Patchwork Materials

Assortment of lightweight fabrics (small prints on cotton are ideal)
Sharp scissors
Newspaper or tissue
Cotton thread
Sharp sewing needles
Medium-weight card
Scalpel or craft knife
Squared paper

First you must decide on your design, either by copying a traditional pattern from a quilting book or by drawing your own design on squared paper. Once you have determined the sizes and shapes of the individual pieces of material to be patched together, you will need to cut a template out of card. To make accurate templates I took an enlarged photocopy of an existing quilt pattern, traced the shape of a segment on to my card and then cut it out. From this template I cut out tissue paper/newspaper equivalents and my pieces of fabric, allowing approximately 0.5cm (¼in) around the edges of the fabric for folding back.

Next I placed my tissue templates against the wrong side of the fabric (checking that the patterning on the fabric lay in the right direction) and turned in and tacked down the edges. I then pressed the sections lightly on the wrong side and removed the papers.

Finally I joined the pieces along the edges, right sides facing each other, using small oversewn stitches.

N.B. These are not, perhaps, the traditional methods of patchwork but for my purposes they seem to work.

If you wish to imitate my designs simply trace the templates given here.

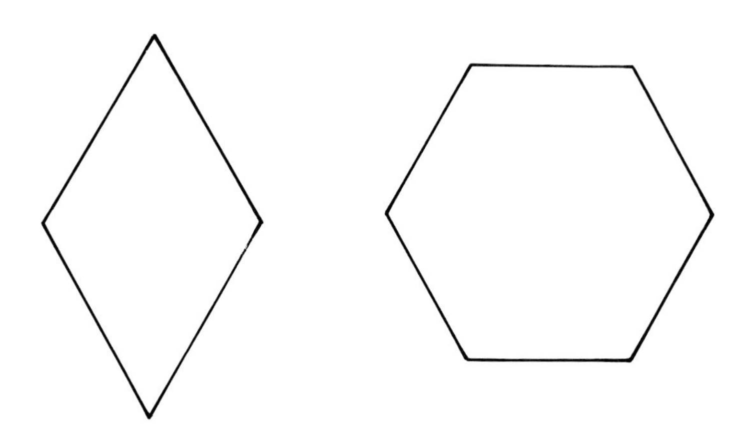

CHRISTMAS HOLLY
I have cheated and stitched these holly appliqués on to a piece of shop-bought black satin quilting. I've added a glitzy bow and have achieved an all-over quilted effect.

Appliqué is the art of applying fabric to fabric and it is a method best embarked upon by those who like to work with a sewing machine.

It is possible to achieve all sorts of interesting effects by cutting out sections of ready-printed fabrics, such as a flower from a chintz print, and by stitching these on to a plain or patterned background to form a new picture.

These cutouts should first be pinned and then tacked, then joined permanently to the background by using a very small zigzag stitch around the edge. This can be played down by using a thread colouring that blends in with your image; alternatively, select a contrasting coloured thread to make a feature of the edging.

If you do not have a sewing machine you can either join the fabrics by hand, using a buttonhole stitch, or work in small overstitches so that your finished work resembles patchwork.

Extra interest can be achieved by padding the piece you intend to appliqué or by adding embroidery, beads or more appliqué to your cutout before applying it to your background.

Appliqué methods are often incorporated into patchwork quilts. By applying a printed image you can turn an abstract patchwork into a pictorial wonder or, on a smaller scale, you can cut and apply plain fabrics in shapes that resemble animals, birds, cups and saucers or what you will. If you cannot find the exact colours you require you can hand-colour pieces of calico with water-based paints or fabric dyes. The first method is suggested on the understanding that the person receiving the card is not likely to throw it in the washing machine along with their precious white undies.

DEAR HEART
This heart was created by Karen Lewis, an extremely talented fabric sculptor. She took her inspiration from a Jammy Dodger biscuit and produced the heart by hand-painting calico and applying embroidery and appliqué to a heart-shaped cutout. She then joined two hearts together with buttonhole stitch, padding them in between. Truly a labour of love!

WORKING WITH

Needles

Needlework is an ideal medium for greeting cards as it allows you to use up all those bits of fancy thread and background fabrics purchased for larger projects.

If your relationship to date with sewing and knitting needles only stretches as far as pricking yourself with one or unblocking the sink with the other, do not despair. Think of all those old but gorgeous jumpers and bits of embroidered fabric that you have lying around, just waiting for a new purpose in life. Jumble and garage sales often throw up some wonderful embroidered doilies from the thirties and forties, which, though unusable in a modern decor, would look charming mounted on greeting cards. You could also use this opportunity to experiment and discover that perhaps you have missed out on a creative and rewarding pastime.

CROSS STITCH AND NEEDLEPOINT

I should warn you that both of these pastimes are extremely addictive and, while they are pitched as being a route to creative expression, I believe that it is the sheer simplicity and repetitiveness of the techniques that make them a wonderfully mindless pleasure at the end of a stressful day. You will need the following materials to design and stitch your own cards:

Cross Stitch Materials

Crewel needles
Evenweave fabric offcuts or custom-made Aida, ideally 14 holes per inch (hpi), or 32-count linen, which produces 16 stitches to the inch
Embroidery cottons: check out the Anchor stranded cotton range or use leftovers
Scissors
Graph paper
Pencil
Eraser
Coloured crayons

To produce your own design, first cut your fabric to fit the selected card mount and count the number of holes both vertically and horizontally that are available to work on through your card window.

N.B. If you are using linen you should stitch over two strands of the linen thread both vertically and horizontally. This means that, when measuring, you should count the threads instead of the holes and then halve the total to establish how many stitches will fit across the row. Draw an outline on your graph paper allowing one square per stitch and draw or trace your design on to this in pencil. Colour in your design and select threads to match your colours. If you are using Anchor stranded cottons use three strands of cotton on 14 hpi Aida and two strands on 18 hpi. Work crosses as per diagrams below but make sure you follow the one golden rule: all your top stitches should slant in the same direction. Work the design from your chart and mount when completed.

You can use my alphabet chart for producing messages or names in lettering. Note that these have been worked on 32-count linen which gives you 16 stitches to the inch. On my Jewish New Year Card (overleaf) I have incorporated gold thread. All the colours quoted are Anchor colours but you can of course use your own selection.

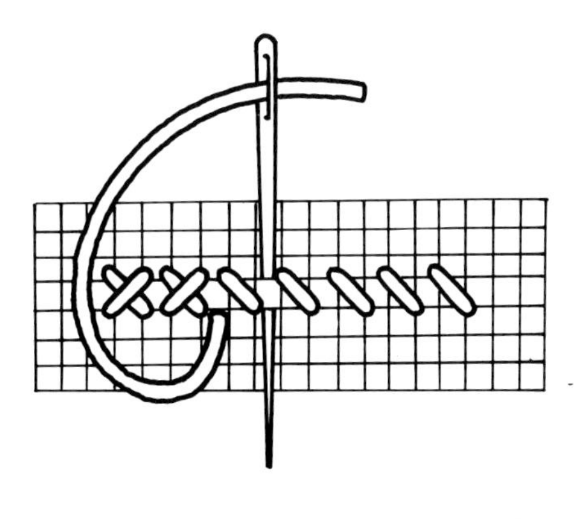

Cross Stitch

THE MESSAGE READS . . .
Use my lettering chart to spell out your own message in cross stitch, even if it's unprintable.

Needlepoint Materials

Tapestry (blunt-ended) needles
Embroidery wools
Tapestry canvas 10, 12 or 14 holes per inch
Paper
Pens
Graph paper etc., as for cross stitch

Use exactly the same design approach as for cross stitch. You will, however, be working your design in half-cross stitch (see diagram) and covering the background area with stitches. I have used needlepoint to make a small card-sized picture frame which I have glued to the front of the card. Write your message within the frame and you have both card and gift in one.

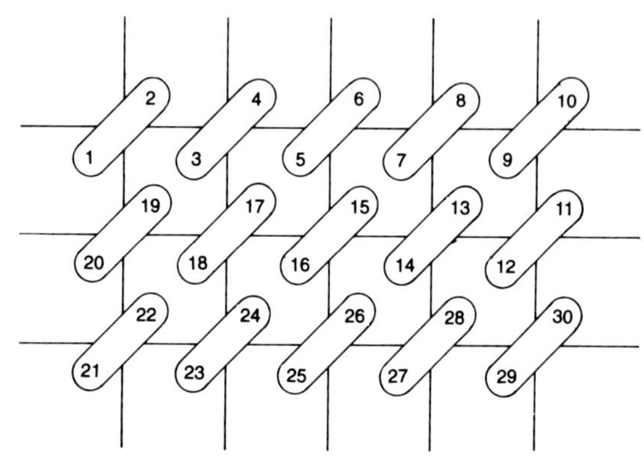

Half Cross Stitch for use in Needlepoint

You can also experiment with a sampler of different stitches using Binca, a 6 hpi canvas usually sold in bright colours and popular with children. You can stitch an assortment of random patterns using soft cottons or wools and the result is bold and attractive.

FRAMED YOU!
Use your needlepoint skills to create this little frame. Glue it to the front of your card and you have a card and gift in one. *(See Frame Chart on p.44.)*

× =131 BLUE
■ =55 PINK
I =256 GREEN
● =936 BROWN
⌝ =304 GOLD (COTTON)
⊥ =295 YELLOW
\/ =GOLD LUREX (FOLLOW ANGLE)

CROSS STITCH ON 14 HOLES PER INCH AIDA

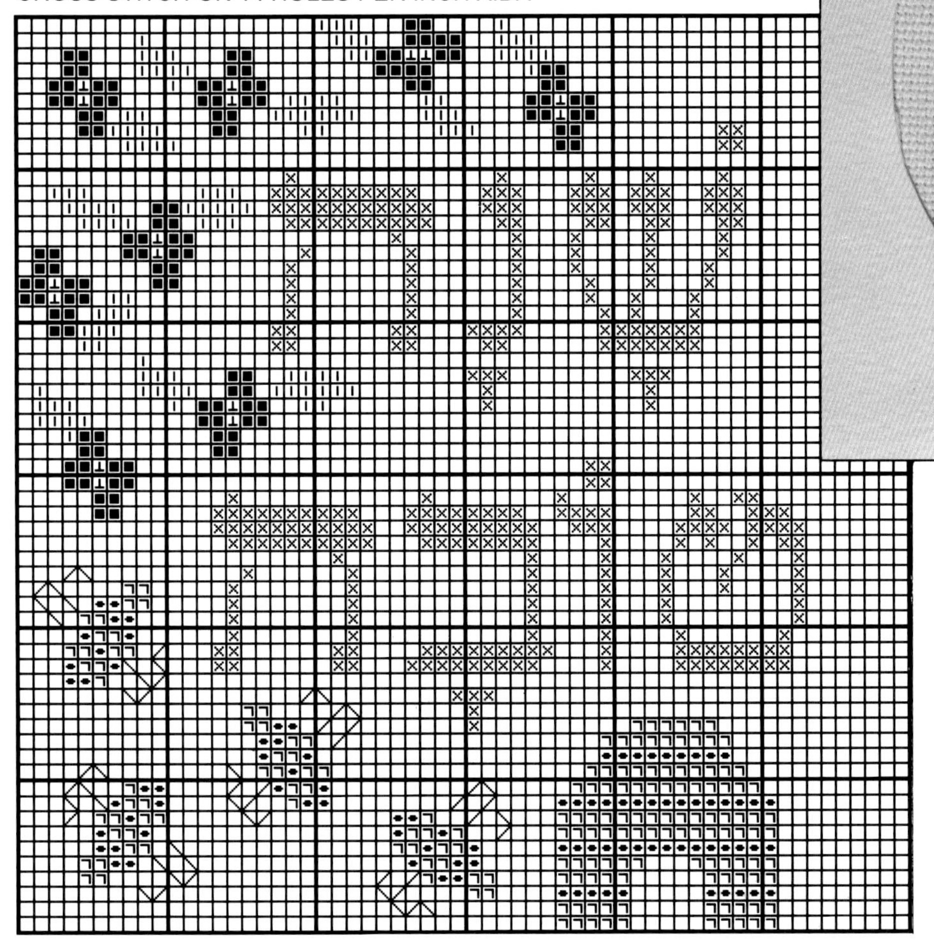

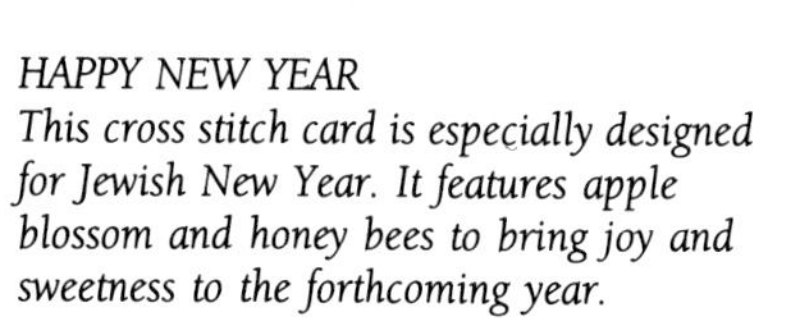

HAPPY NEW YEAR
This cross stitch card is especially designed for Jewish New Year. It features apple blossom and honey bees to bring joy and sweetness to the forthcoming year.

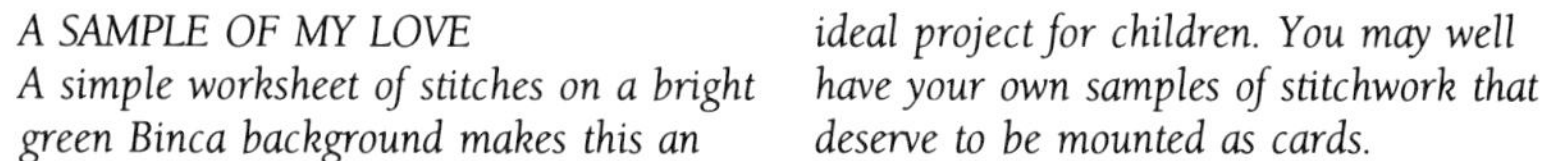

A SAMPLE OF MY LOVE
A simple worksheet of stitches on a bright green Binca background makes this an ideal project for children. You may well have your own samples of stitchwork that deserve to be mounted as cards.

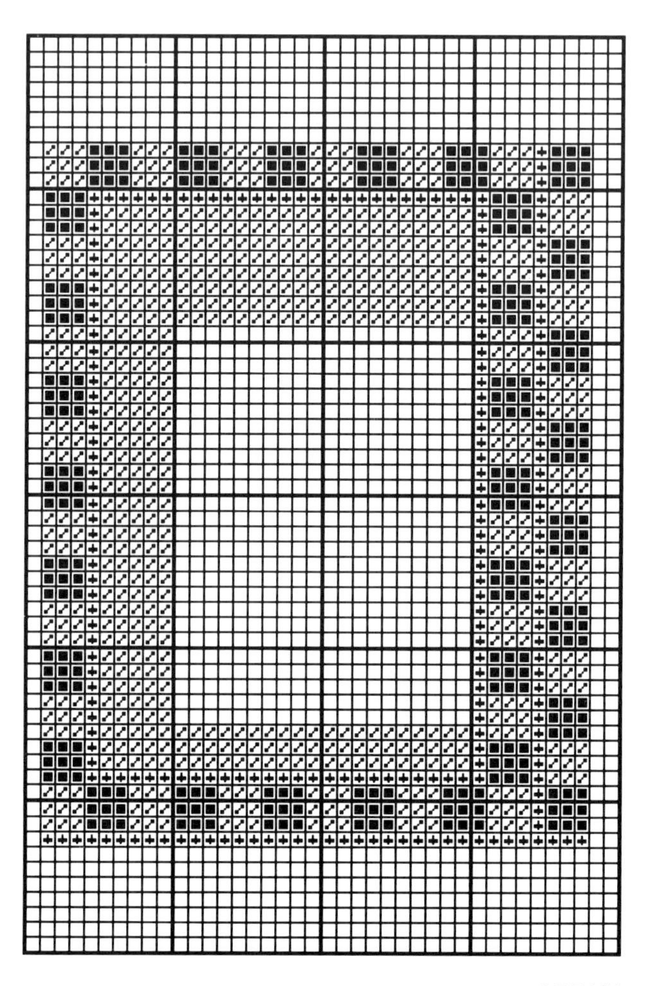

FRAMED YOU

EMBROIDERY

If you have even the most basic knowledge of embroidery and a supply of offcuts of linen or other interesting fabrics, you can create some very pretty greeting cards.

My crinoline lady was traced from an old forties needlework book and is worked in straight stitch, cross stitch, buttonhole stitch, stem stitch and lazy daisy. Straight stitch is just as it sounds and details of cross stitch are given on p.41. Follow the diagrams below to master the other stitches I have used.

You can trace any clear image and outline it in straight stitch or stem stitch and you could personalize the card by including the embroidered name of the recipient or a message of greeting.

My harvest mouse (see p.46) is worked over two layers of fabric with some wadding in between to create a slightly quilted effect.

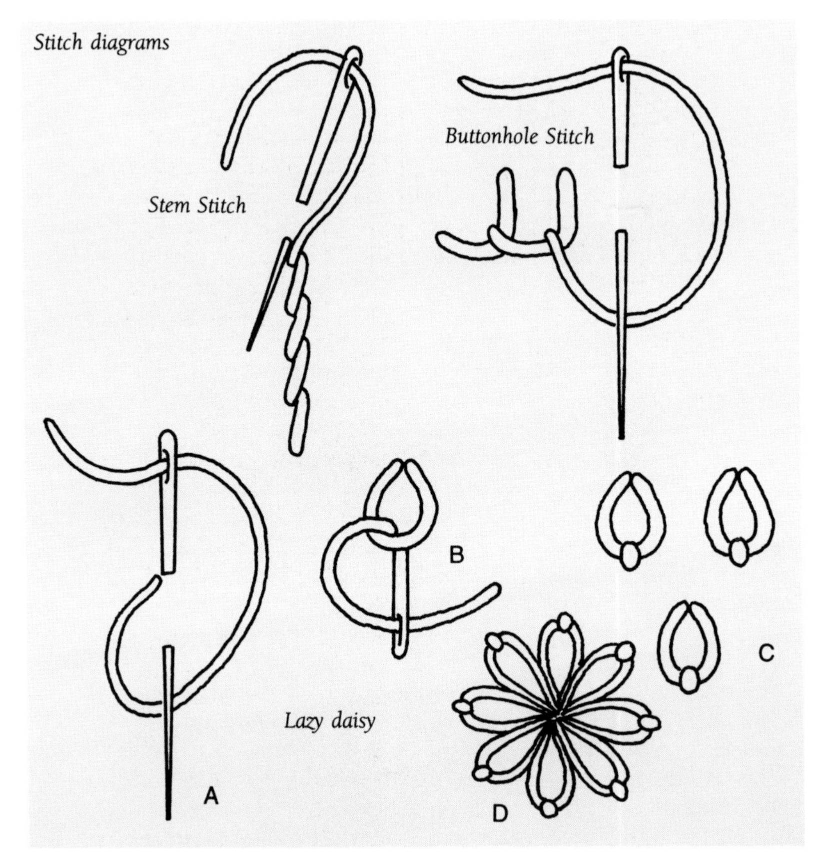

MARY, MARY, QUITE CONTRARY
You don't need to know much about embroidery to make this pretty card for a daughter's or mother's birthday. To add dimension you could frame it with a lace trim, preferably one you have made yourself.

HARVEST MOUSE
Happy Thanksgiving. This little mouse sits in a quilted field and is worked on linen. He would look just as good sitting on a hessian background or a patchwork field.

KNITTING AND CROCHET

It would be silly to attempt to teach you to knit and crochet for the purpose of making greeting cards. Life is too short. If, however, you have mastered the very basics in knitting, i.e. casting-on and garter stitch, you can make either my teddy's jumper or my stripey scarf by following the instructions below. On the other hand, if you are a serious knitter, you are bound to have drawers full of tension swatches that you have been wondering what to do with; card-making is the perfect way to give them a second life.

When selecting swatches for mounting I suggest you use only those knitted in 2-, 3- or 4-ply wool or cotton since anything heavier tends to look ungainly. If you have lacy swatches, these are ideal and look very pretty mounted on a contrasting background. Bobbly swatches in bright colours are also fun used either on their own or as part of a fabric collage. Traditional Fair Isle designs look delicious mounted and I am including a chart for one of my favourites. You can select soft pretty colours, sharp primaries or earthy shades depending on who the card is for. Crochet swatches can be used in the same way as knitted ones.

To make my Teddy jumper (on p.48) simply cut out head, legs and hands from yellow felt and draw on the facial features with a felt-tipped pen. Position these felt cutouts on your card using the photograph as a guide and glue down with a rubber-based adhesive. Cut a bow-tie shape from a contrasting scrap of felt.

For the jumper I have used an oddment of mohair and some $3^{3}/_{4}$mm knitting needles. Cast on 12 stitches in your main colour (A) and knit 1 row. Changing to a contrast (B), knit 2 rows. Back to A, knit 2 rows. Back to B, knit 2 rows. Change to A and cast on 6 stitches at the beginning of the next 2 rows. Continue in stripe sequence for a further 7 rows. Cast off. Glue jumper over Teddy's hands, legs and head. Glue on bow-tie.

For the miniature scarf I have used oddments of 4-ply knitting cotton which I have knitted on normal $2^{3}/_{4}$mm needles and then slid on to the miniature needles when complete. Cast on 12 stitches and knit every row in a stripe sequence of your choice for 20 rows. Slip these stitches on to a double-ended needle. Cut the pointed ends off two cocktail sticks with a pair of scissors and glue on two wooden beads. Slide an equal number of stitches on to each 'needle' and mount your knitting on to a card with a rubber-based adhesive.

For the Fair Isle swatch opposite you will need oddments of red, navy, white, yellow and grey 4-ply wool and some 3mm needles. Cast on 19 stitches in grey and then follow the chart in stocking stitch (knit one row, purl the next) until the chart is complete. Cast off.

N.B. Strand the colours not in use across the back of your work.

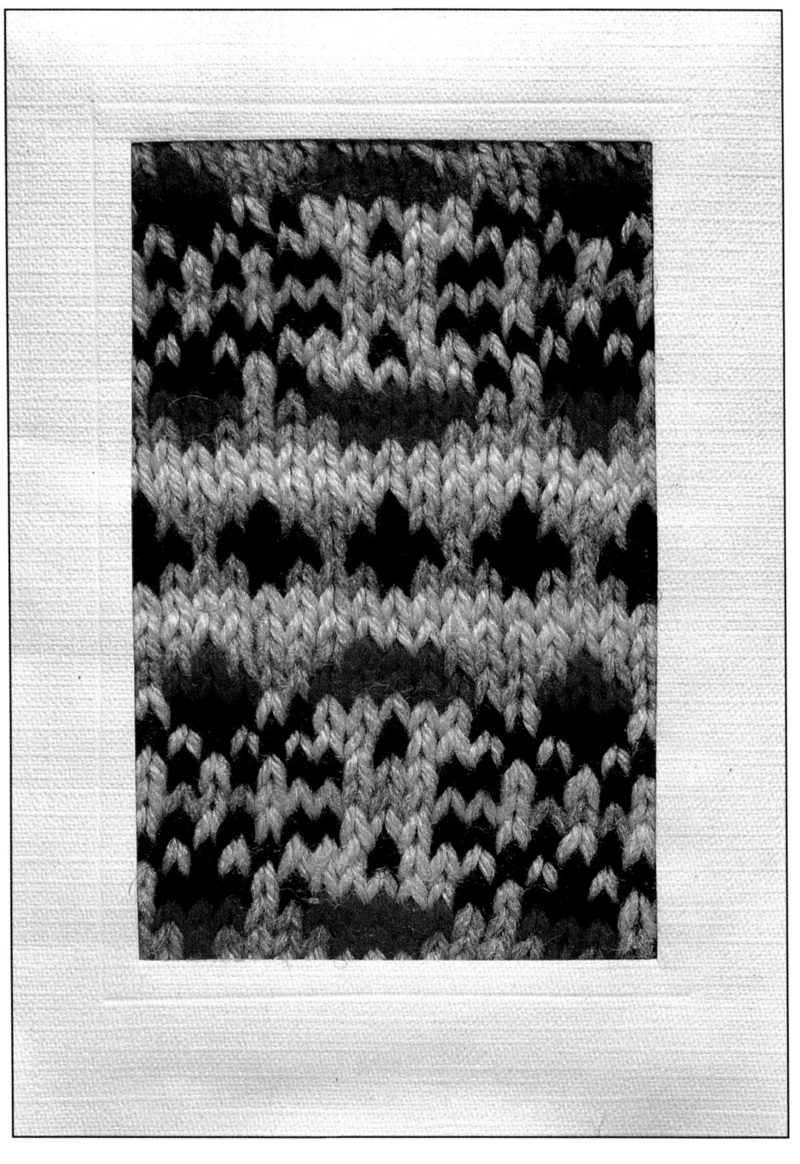

I COULDN'T MANAGE THE WHOLE JUMPER . . .
So you sent your dad/husband/boyfriend a little bit of Fair Isle. At least he doesn't have to worry about the sleeves being different lengths!

Mount the card as required.

If you can produce a simple chain and double chain stitch, you can make the pretty flowers behind my louvred shutters (on p.48). Having never attempted crochet before I managed to create these by making a chain and joining it back on itself to form leaves then turning it back to the centre for each petal. I have used a fine crochet hook and shiny embroidery cottons and silks to complete my card, but you could use wools if you prefer.

The crochet garden has an assortment of seven flowers in cottons and silks. I have used a basic window template (see p.88) and have then cut a sheet of white textured paper to the size of the front of the card. In pencil, draw a rectangle in the centre of the card, leaving a 2.5cm (1in) margin around the edges; then draw a vertical line through the middle of this rectangle. With a craft knife, cut horizontally along the top and bottom of this central rectangle and then down the vertical line. Crease and fold back along the left and right sides of the rectangle to form window shutters.

In the centre of each shutter, draw rectangles in pencil, approximately 0.5 cm (¼in) from the edge. Pencil in horizontal lines approximately 0.5 cm (¼in) apart down these inner rectangles and carefully slit them with your craft knife to form louvre slats. Make vertical cuts upwards from the end of each of these to about half the depth of each slat. Draw on gold window knobs with a felt-tipped pen. Glue the textured paper with shutters over your basic window card.

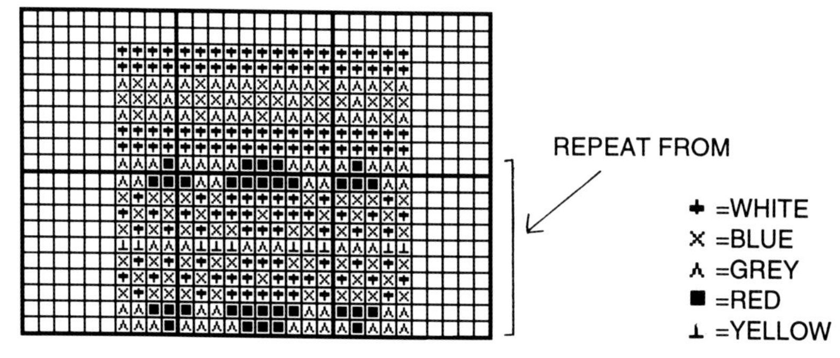

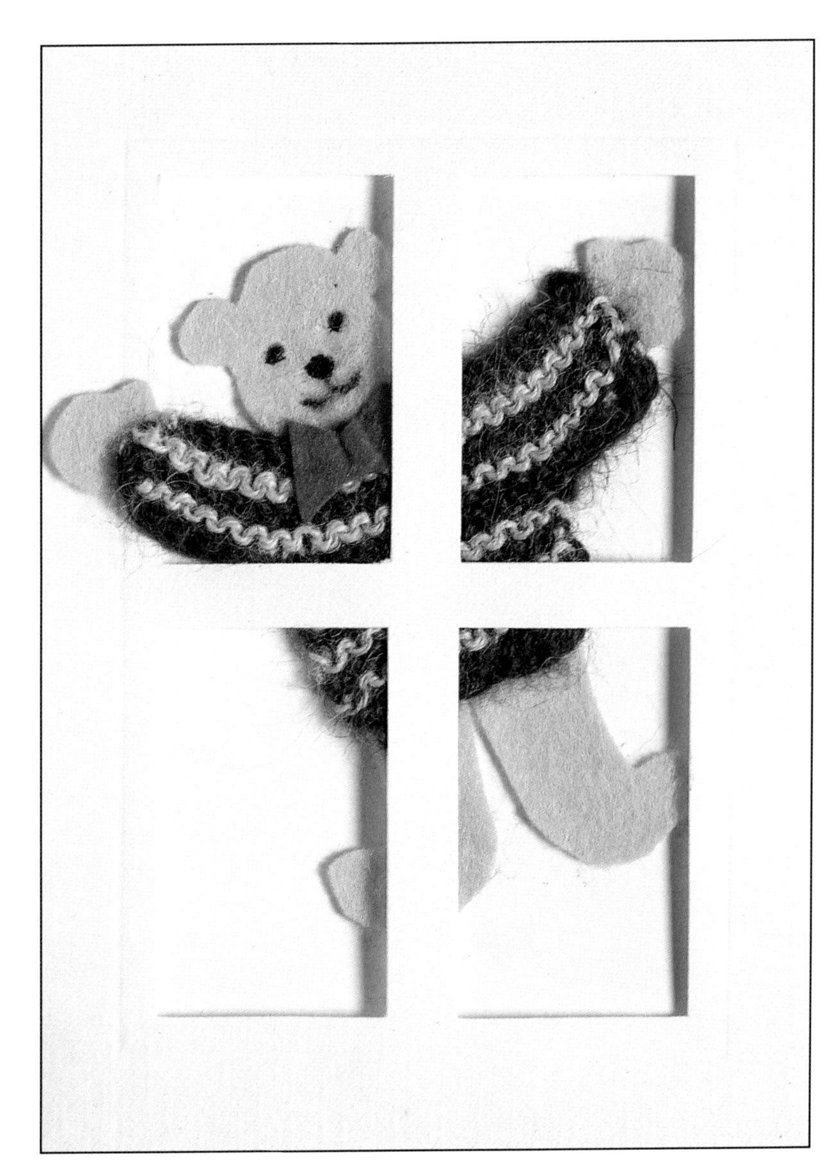

I LOVE YOU THIS MUCH
This bear is cut from felt and is wearing a simple garter stitch jumper. A good children's project.

SNUG AS A BUG
A cheerful scarf for a very small person or perhaps a card for Grandma's birthday.

SPRING HAS SPRUNG
Little crochet flowers can be made from a simple crochet chain. You could hide these behind a louvred window or simply arrange them prettily on the background of your choice.

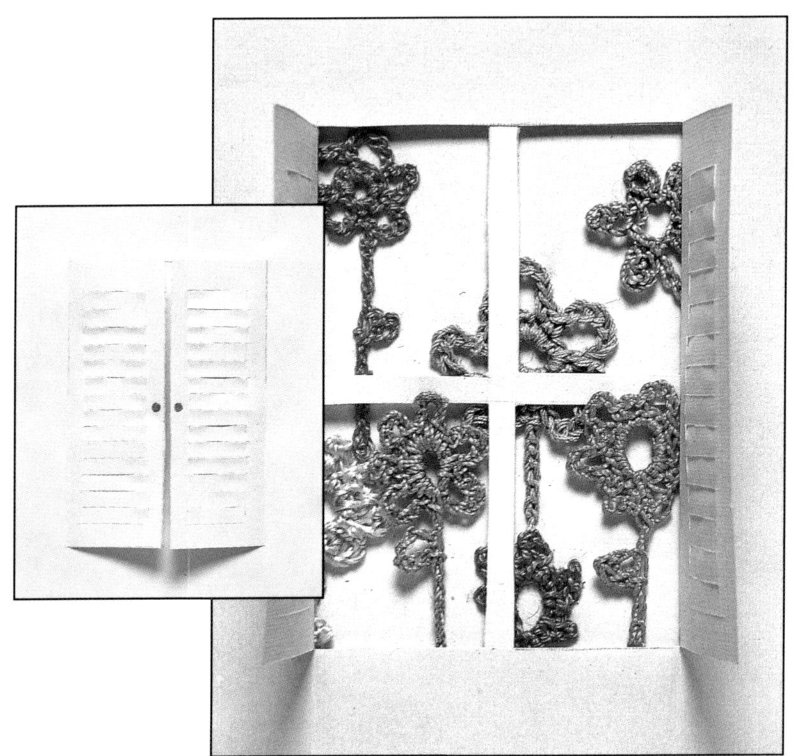

WORKING WITH

Dough

Doughcraft is wonderful rainy-day fun for all the family and you will be surprised at all the different things you can make with the minimum of skill. You can dry dough in a normal oven to a rock-hard finish or, on a warm day, you can even dry it in the sun. You can paint the finished pieces using water-based paints or felt-tipped pens, and with a coat of varnish your creation will have a professional finish that will look like pottery.

For those who cannot be bothered with dough, all the following projects can be produced with FIMO, a modelling material clay that can be oven-dried and painted. FIMO is available in a number of colours in addition to white, so you can get some very clever results without even touching a paintbrush.

Materials

Basic dough ingredients i.e. flour, water, salt, cooking oil
Water-based acrylic paints
Varnish (optional)
Paintbrushes
Clear glue
Fine sandpaper
Safety pins
Cocktail stick or knitting needle (to assist with modelling)
Bottle and jar tops in various sizes
Pastry cutters in various shapes
Garlic crusher
Ribbons for medal and balloon strings

Dough Recipe

To make around twenty cards (halve or quarter my quantities if you just want to make a small number of cards).

2 cups (8oz/225g) plain flour
1 cup (4oz/110g) salt
1 cup water
1 tbsp cooking oil

Mix all the ingredients together and knead until the dough has a soft, smooth consistency. If it is too dry, add a little oil; if too gritty, knead it some more, as the salt hasn't been properly absorbed.

All the projects in this book were made up either with balls of dough of various sizes, rolled round and round on a table until smooth, or with 'snakes' of dough, rolled into tubes with the palm of the hand then cut into various lengths. Pieces are joined together by wetting and pressing gently into position and features were added with the assistance of a sharp cocktail stick or knitting needle. For hair, try pressing a ball of dough through a garlic crusher and for badges in various shapes and sizes you can use pre-shaped pastry cutters, bottle tops or whatever comes to hand in the shape you want to achieve.

When you have completed your masterpiece put it in the oven at the very lowest setting and leave it for around six hours. Alternatively, leave a tray of finished items in an airing cupboard or similar warm place until it is completely dry. Test for dryness by pushing a needle into it – this should not be possible.

Troubleshooting

If bits fall off during the drying process you can glue them on again. If the dough cracks during baking the oven temperature is too high. Lower it and stick the figure together again by wetting the bits that should join each other and pressing them into place.

Decorating

Smooth off any lumpy bits with very fine sandpaper then paint with acrylic paints. Work one colour at a time, letting this dry thoroughly before adding the next one. When your painting is complete you can varnish the finished item to get a clear shiny finish.

CHRISTMAS WREATH
This little wreath was made by plaiting together three snakes of dough and decorating with small balls of dough. After baking and painting you can highlight the decorations with gold felt-tipped pen or glitter. Glue to your card with clear adhesive.

40 TODAY
And you deserve a medal for getting there! Roll dough ½cm (¼in) thick and cut out a circle with a jar top. Cut a snake and form the numbers, then moisten the back and press carefully on to your disc. Bake as per instructions and decorate as you will. Glue on to a length of ribbon like a medal and glue a safety pin on the back. Attach to card.

LITTLE TED
Child's party invitation or placecard. Ted is made from four balls of dough (body, head and two ears) and a snake cut into four lengths for his arms and legs. Join arms at shoulders, flattening slightly, and press paws into shape. Carefully moisten and press on ears. Bake and paint yellow. Add features and bow tie with fine paintbrush and glue to card. You could also stick a safety pin on the back so that Ted can double as a badge when the party is over.

SIX TODAY
To make this little boy, roll a ball of dough for his tummy and a slightly smaller one for his head, then press together. Cut a snake in four and add as legs and arms. Cut a small piece of snake in half and press this along his head for hair, add a small blob of dough for nose, make hair by scoring dough with a cocktail stick; bake and dress with the help of paint. Glue two narrow ribbons on your card topped with two fluorescent rounds of paper for balloons. Add a strip of green paper for grass.

LOVE AND KISSES
These lips were made with simple cut snakes of dough pressed together to form lips of slightly different shapes and sizes. The heart is ½cm (¼in) thick dough cut out freehand or using a heart-shaped pastry cutter.

TO MY PRINCESS
The curtains on this card have been drawn with a silver felt-tipped pen. The ballerina consists of one snake of dough for the body, scored down the leg areas to form a division and pressed together at the feet to form points. Add a ball of dough on top for head and two smaller balls of dough for breasts. Add one snake cut in two equal lengths for arms (flattened at the end to form hands). Bake, paint and leave to dry. To make the dress, fold a 10cm (4in) length of voile ribbon or net in half and run a thread through the two long edges. Pull into a gather and glue at waist. Add a bow at the waist and a ribbon rose in her hair. Glue to card.

BE MINE
This figure was made in exactly the same way as the ballerina except without the breasts. He is mounted on painted corrugated card and his flowers are scrunched-up pieces of crepe paper in a tissue paper wrapping. The moon is cut from hologram paper and the grass is green crepe paper sprinkled with silver glitter.

WELCOME TO THE WORLD
This card for a new arrival was made with a 2.5cm (1in) diameter roll of dough flattened for the baby's back and scored with a cocktail stick to form the legs. A snake cut in two equal lengths forms the arms and balls of dough have been pushed on for the head, hands, buttocks and feet. The hair was made by pushing a small ball of dough through a garlic crusher. The rainbow is overlays of gummed paper in bright colours fanned on to a silver card.

Painting

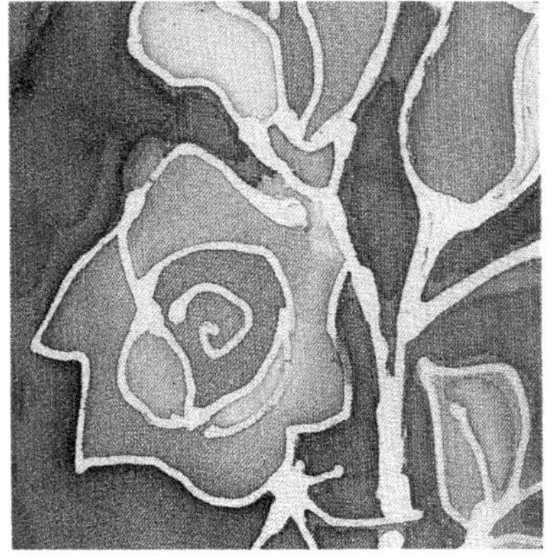

While I have tried throughout this book to inspire you with alternative materials for your greeting cards, painted and printed cards remain the most practical in terms of their 'mailability'; these are also the most suitable methods to use if you wish to duplicate a design.

What should be emphasized is the fact that you do not need art-school skills to produce an attractive card. Painting, to my mind, is simply a question of applying your paints to card, whatever the method, and creating an interesting arrangement of colours. The most impressive results are usually achieved by accident so arm yourself with some basic colours and bits and bobs and experiment.

Materials

Water-based paints in bold colours usually give you the best results. Acrylic paints are wonderful because you can splodge them on with a palette knife and produce textured results and water-based inks give you strong clear colours. For the methods used here you will need a small collection of brushes, both pointed and flat-ended, plus some drinking straws, a pot of water, egg cups or baby-food jars, and card in colours of your choice.

FIREWORKS
Always good for celebrations. Add some glitter streaks for special effect.

STRAW BLOWING

This is great fun for both adults and children although you must take care not to drink your paint. Mix about 2.5cm (1in) of tubed paint with half an egg cup full of water, insert your straw, suck slightly and then blow your paint on the card. Leave this to dry for a minute while you prepare the next colour and continue until you are happy with the results.

FLOWER POWER
A brush technique for non-painters. Why not make up one enormous flower-head to create a kaleidoscope effect?

SPLATTERING

This is self-explanatory. Simply fill your brush-head with paint and either run your finger back through it or jog the brush towards the card so the paint splatters over the surface.

All of the above methods not only form attractive images in their own right but can also be used on a card window surround to give you a background for another medium.

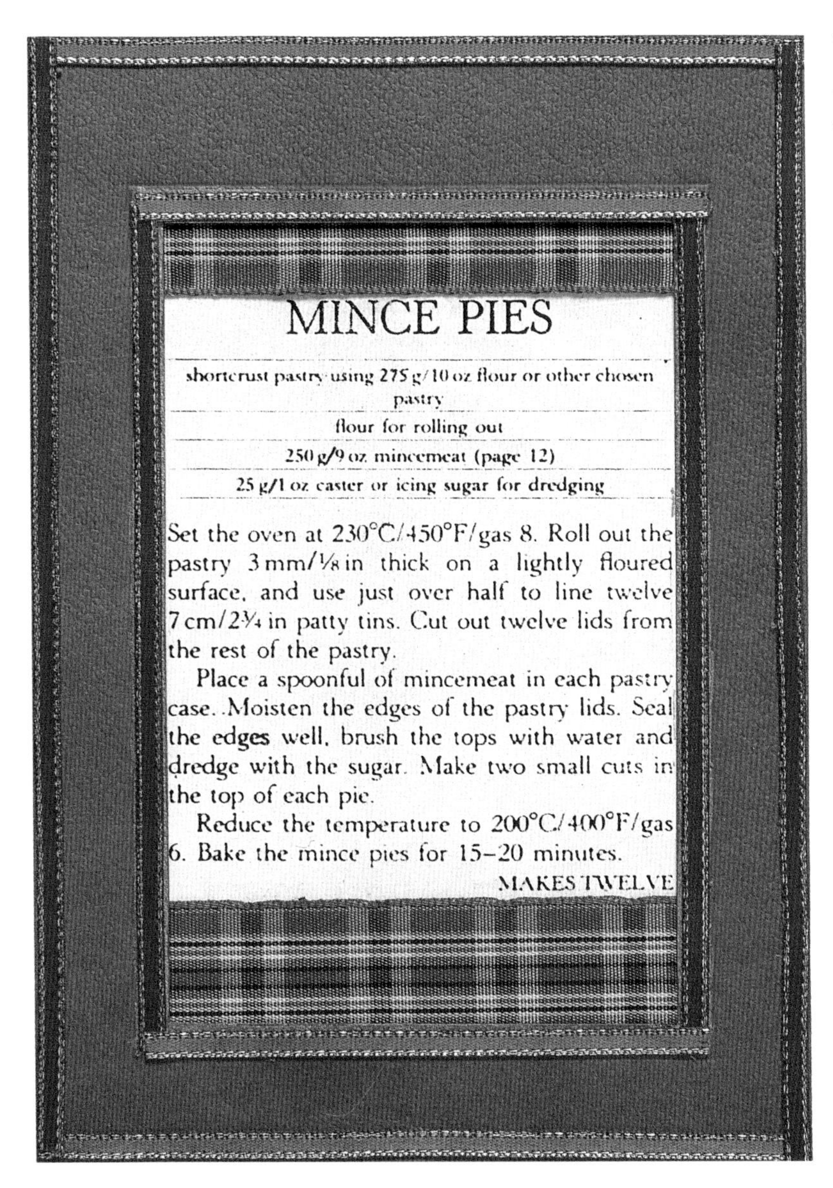

MINCE PIES

shortcrust pastry using 275 g/10 oz flour or other chosen pastry

flour for rolling out

250 g/9 oz mincemeat (page 12)

25 g/1 oz caster or icing sugar for dredging

Set the oven at 230°C/450°F/gas 8. Roll out the pastry 3 mm/⅛ in thick on a lightly floured surface, and use just over half to line twelve 7 cm/2¾ in patty tins. Cut out twelve lids from the rest of the pastry.

Place a spoonful of mincemeat in each pastry case. Moisten the edges of the pastry lids. Seal the edges well, brush the tops with water and dredge with the sugar. Make two small cuts in the top of each pie.

Reduce the temperature to 200°C/400°F/gas 6. Bake the mince pies for 15–20 minutes.

MAKES TWELVE

MINCE PIES
A Christmas recipe, photocopied, mounted and framed with ribbon. You could photocopy any news item or wedding announcement that you think is particularly amusing or appropriate.

BRUSH STROKES

By using your brush in different ways you can achieve some strong abstract images. Flower Power was created by dipping a flat-ended brush in red watercolour and laying the flat of the brush on to a card, positioning each dab to form a circle. When dry, the area between was filled with mauve or yellow. The stems, leaves and flower centres were made with little dabs, holding the brush upright so that only the very top of the hairs on the brush touched the card.

SPONGING

This method will provide you with a softer, pretty effect and you will get the best results with a natural sponge. Mix your paints as described for straw blowing, or use inks. Dip your sponge into the paint, squeeze out the excess and dab your card with the colour of your choice.

PAINTING PRINTED IMAGES

If you can't draw, but want to achieve more formal results, your best resource is your local photocopy shop. These days copiers can print on virtually any paper and can provide you with interesting outlines which you can then colour in.

Create a basic black outline by tracing around an image from a magazine or a child's colouring book. Photocopy this on to the paper of your choice – brown wrapping paper gives interesting results – and colour in. You can also highlight your design with gold or silver felt-tips or add texture with some of the new special effect pens that will produce an embossed finish.

Photocopiers are also useful for reproducing recipes or appropriate household hints which can then be mounted on card and framed with ribbon. See my Mince Pie card.

MARBLING

This is a traditional skill which relies on the resistance between oil and water. For finely marbled designs, oil-based colours, mixed with cooking oil, turpentine and washing-up liquid, are floated on the surface of a tray of water and then agitated or combed to form interesting patterns. A sheet of paper is then laid on top of the water and lifted off, so transferring the paint to the paper.

You will need to play about with different quantities of oil, turpentine and washing-up liquid to achieve a consistency of paint that will float on top of the water. If the paint is too thick it will sink, so add washing up liquid/turpentine. If the colour is too thin it will not show up, so add more colour.

For stronger or more controlled designs you can also float your oil-based paints or inks on size: i.e. add wallpaper paste to your water using approximately one heaped tablespoon of paste to one litre (1¾ pints/four cups) of water.

BRIGHT AND BEAUTIFUL
This interesting marbled effect has been achieved by floating oil paints on top of size and lifting the image off the surface of the size with the paper.

MY HEART GOES WITH YOU
Professional designer and card-maker Debbie Harter has produced this card with a photocopier. The shapes were drawn freestyle, copied and then coloured in.

PAINTING ON SILK

Painting on silk is a great deal easier than it looks. Indeed, some of the new products on the market make it almost idiot-proof (except for the odd splodge here and there . . .). It is also a technique that will lead you on to bigger and better things since once you have mastered the silk-painted greeting card you may well find yourself making a scarf, then a cushion, and before you know it both you and your home will be completely decorated with silk paintings of your very own creation.

You will need to invest in the following equipment, but when considering the cost, bear in mind the number of cards you will be able to produce from it.

Materials

A set of water-based silk paints – Marabu are wonderful
A tube of contour lining medium or gutta (blocking agent to stop colours running into each other; it comes in a special dispenser)
A length of white or cream silk, fine cotton or synthetic material
Paint brushes
Jar of water
Ironing board and iron
Drawing pins or tacks

If you are going to take this seriously, you will need a wooden frame (a picture frame will do, or four pieces of 5cm (2in) square battening, nailed together). For greeting cards, however, you can use an embroidery hoop to keep the fabric taut.

STAINED-GLASS WINDOW
An easy card to start with. Divide your silk into panes of glass with your gutta and blob in some interesting colours. Mount in an arched frame.

Instructions

1. First hand-wash your silk in hand-warm water and mild detergent to remove any dressing. Rinse and roll in a towel. When still damp, iron at a low setting.
2. Stretch silk on to frame and tack at 2.5cm (1in) intervals. Alternatively place in embroidery hoop, making sure that the fabric is taut.
3. (Gutta method.) Sketch your design with a contour pen or gutta dispenser. If you don't feel you can draw well enough, outline an existing design on paper in black pen, place this under the framed silk and simply trace it on to the silk with your contour pen or gutta. Leave to dry for ten minutes.
4. With a paintbrush, colour in with silk paints, which can be mixed in the same way as watercolours.
5. When your design is dry, remove it from the frame and iron it on the wrong side, with the iron set at the cotton temperature, to fix.
6. Wash out the gutta lines by placing the ironed painting in cold water. Roll in a towel then iron damp at low temperature.
7. Mount on card with a rubber-based glue, glueing around the edges only.

The gutta will divide your colours with a white line. If you want the colours to run into each other in an abstract fashion do not use it; just paint directly on to the pre-washed silk. If you leave the paint to dry you can then highlight areas with a fine brush or pen.

CONGRATULATIONS
A bouquet of silk flowers. The gutta divisions give it a stencilled look. Pretty for any occasion.

CHRISTMAS CANDLE
The natural colour-blends of the silk paint add a realistic glow to this candle image. Drawn using the gutta technique.

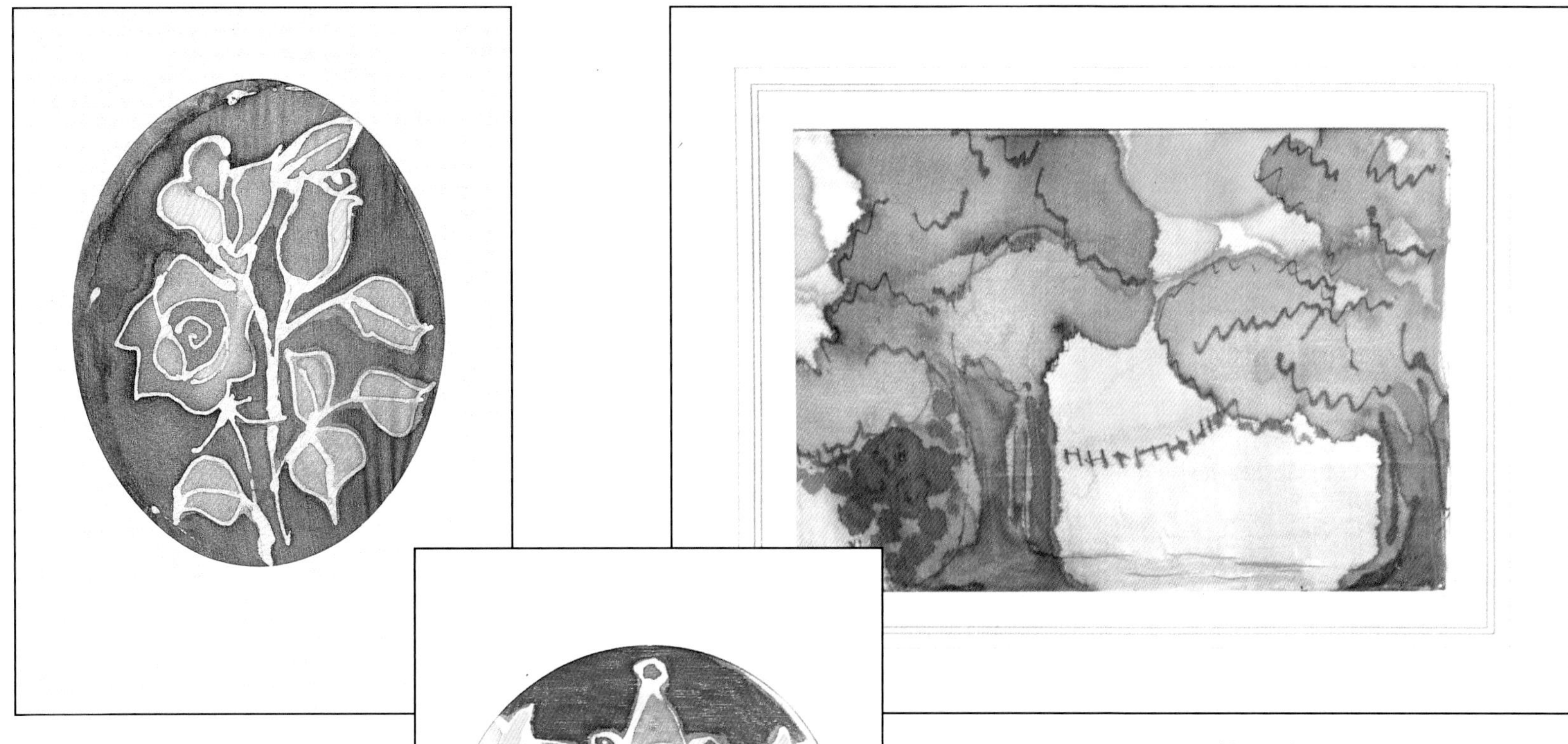

ANNIVERSARY ROSES
I drew this freestyle, not quite knowing what I wanted to achieve. A few swirls of gutta quickly suggested a rose, and by watering down the paint I got the shaded effect of the petals. The background was added last. Someone once told me that embroidery and art existed to correct nature's imperfections. I strongly disagree – if it's perfect, it's boring.

HAPPY DAYS
This design is gutta-less. Simply blob on the paint, let it run and see what the image suggests to you. Then highlight your thoughts with black or brown ink.

CLOWN AROUND ON YOUR BIRTHDAY
A jolly Mr Clown for the kids, sketched with gutta and filled in with bright colours.

Printing

You do not need a printing press to print cards. Printed images can be created with potatoes, string, leaves, corks or indeed any piece of household equipment with an interesting shape and/or texture that you happen to have lying around. If you want to produce a run of cards, arm yourself with the following tools and have a go at printing.

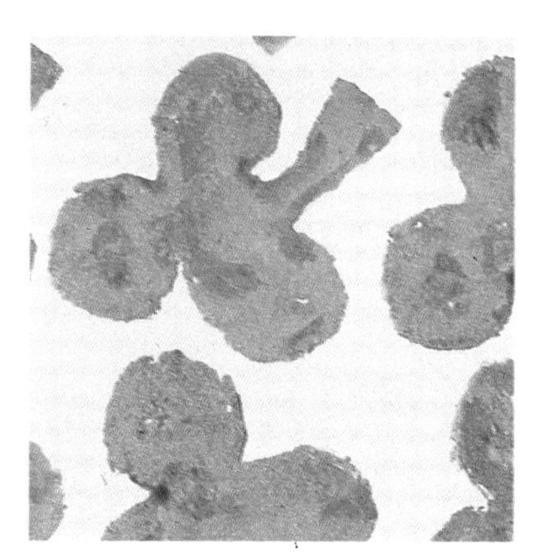

Materials

Roller
Water-based inks
Piece of glass
Craft knife
Kitchen paper
A saucer or empty tin
Pencils
Felt-tipped pens
Items you wish to print with, e.g. potatoes, erasers, string, card etc.

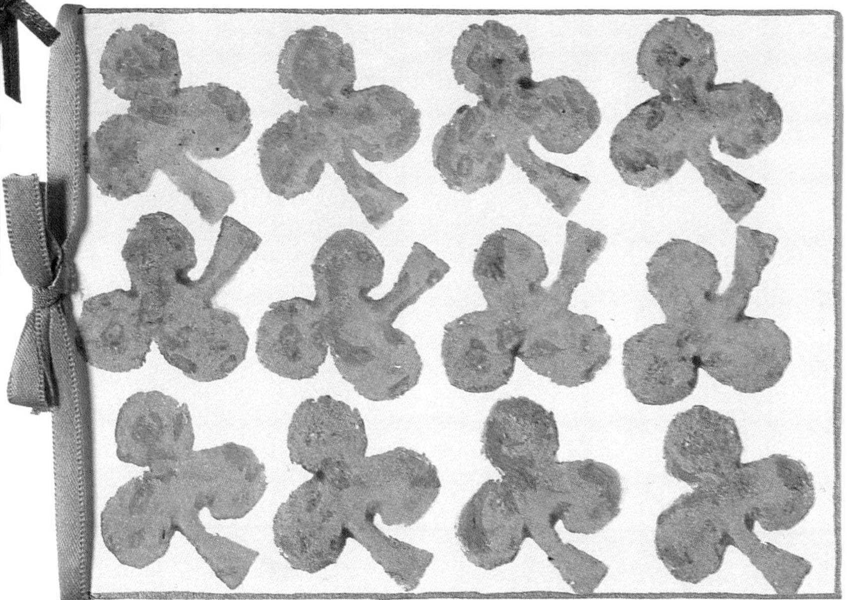

BE MY TRUE LOVE
A simple potato print using red and orange. A perfect project for children.

HAPPY ST PATRICK'S DAY
What can be more appropriate than making a St Patrick's Day card with a potato print of a shamrock?

POTATO PRINTS

Clever little printing blocks can be made by carving potatoes and stamping your design on to card using water-based inks.

Cut the potato in half and draw on your design. (N.B. Make sure you always draw lettering back-to-front to print it the right way round.) Either work with a mirror or trace your lettering and use the reverse side. With your craft knife carve this design in relief. The most successful potato prints result from using simple shapes creatively positioned on your page. Dry the face of the potato with kitchen paper before inking it, as you will not get a clear image if it is too moist. Make an ink stamp by folding up some kitchen paper, cotton wool or felt and saturating it with ink. If you keep this in a tin it will last for future projects. Potato cuts can be kept for a few days if wrapped in plastic and stored in the refrigerator. Wash the potato thoroughly before moving on to a new colour.

LOVE AND FISHES OR HEARTS AND HERRINGS
A bright and cheerful notelet, printed on textured paper. Make yourself a dozen or so.

STRING PRINTS

Glue different types of string, wool and thread on to a card to make a design. Pour some ink on to a sheet of glass and roll it with your roller until it is evenly coated, then roll on to the string and card printing block. Now take a piece of paper and place it over the block and either press firmly all over with your fist or use a clean roller to press the paper on to the block, being careful not to let the paper shift. Peel off and leave to dry.

CARD PRINTS

Cut cardboard shapes to make your design. Interesting effects can be achieved by using corrugated card or punch holes in your picture. Arrange carefully and glue on to card base. Ink up as for string, and print.

ERASER PRINTS

You can print using any old erasers and a rubber stamp pad, or better still, use novelty shapes which you can buy very cheaply from stationery shops. Simply press the eraser on to the pad and print.

LINO PRINTS

Some intricate designs can be achieved using lino tiles and gouges which can be purchased at an art shop. Draw the design on to the lino and cut out the areas you do not wish to see printed with ink. Take great care when gouging out the lino to push the tool away from you; to stop it from slipping, make a wooden frame and clamp it to your work table. To make a frame you will need a piece of wood (an old bread board would be perfect) and a strip of approximately 2.5cm x 2.5cm (1in x 1in) wood the same size or bigger than your lino tile. Nail the strip of wood to the back, upper edge of your bread board to act as a stop. Roll ink and print as described in the string technique.

YOU'RE STRINGING ME ALONG!
Two friendly dolphins, printed from string and having a whale of a time.

HEADING FOR EXTINCTION
This printing block is made from cutouts of card glued on to a base card, in other word a stencil in reverse. You then roll the ink over your design with a roller and press your card on top to create an impression. Both the print and the original printing block will make interesting cards.

WELCOME TO YOUR NEW HOME
This castle is printed from erasers dipped in ink. The door is printed with the side of a ruler and the door studs with the end of a pencil.

PURPLE PUSSYCAT
I also have a red one, a green one and a black one. Lino printing is a good medium to use if you want to make a run of cards.

HAPPY BIRTHDAY
Cut a back-to-front lettering message from cardboard and mount it on card so you can keep it for re-use.

Mixed Bag

There is no limit to the items you can use to decorate greeting cards. This section concentrates on dried flowers, buttons, braids, and bits and bobs.

Once you are hooked on card-making you will find yourself saving all sorts of oddments that you would once have thrown away. If they can be re-used to brighten someone's day, it's a vast improvement on adding to the waste mountain.

DRIED FLOWERS AND LEAVES

Dried flowers have been used in the making of greeting cards for centuries but my ace helper and friend, Judy Newman, has come up with some ideas of her own which I thought should be included in this book. In addition to drying and pressing flowers from hedgerows, she has also made use of shop-bought pot-pourri (available at any time of the year), leaves, moss and even corn. We are in the lucky position of living in the middle of the countryside, but your local park or woodland is sure to provide you with lots of materials to work with if you use Judy's designs for inspiration.

Materials

Tweezers
Scalpel or craft knife
Rubber based glue
Blotting paper
Scissors
Cocktail sticks
Sheet of clear acetate (to protect your finished design)
Heavy books or flower press

Hints and Tips

1. Pick flowers early in the morning when they have just opened. Only use the best specimens; tatty flowers make tatty cards. Do not pick flowers when they are wet, as wet flowers tend to go mouldy during the pressing process.

2. Experiment with a variety of flowers every year and make a list of the ones that press successfully.

3. Splice thick flower head backs and stems. It doesn't matter if the flower heads fall to pieces; they can always be repaired when they are glued on.

4. Do not try to press fleshy petals and leaves since these contain too much water and lose their shape and colour during the pressing process.

5. If you do not have a flower press, lay flowers between two pieces of blotting paper or nappy liners. Place under a pile of heavy books. The drying time is around six weeks (three weeks if you use nappy liners). Do not overcrowd the flowers as they will take longer to dry.

FOR A BOOKWORM
A card that doubles as a bookmark with the rhyme:
'These little flowers placed in your book
Will serve to show you where to look'.

A CORNY CARD
Made from real corn with the mouse and grasses cut from dried leaves.

PEACE AND GOODWILL
This wreath is made by glueing a mixture of dried clover heads, baby fir cones and moss on to a ring of card. All the ingredients with the exception of the moss were taken from a shop-bought pot-pourri mixture.

PAPERAZZI
This little fern is glued to a piece of muslin and then coated with a rubber-based adhesive. It is mounted on a card made from handmade paper which has had flowers added to the pulp during the making process.

When making your card, position the dried flowers in an attractive arrangement and glue down each petal using the tiniest dab of glue (enough to fit on a pin head). You will find it easiest to handle the flowers with tweezers.

When the design is complete, it is advisable to glue a sheet of acetate behind the card window to protect your flower arrangement.

In several of these designs Judy has used leaves, cut into interesting shapes or left whole; these should be treated in the same manner as flowers. She has also used corn heads and you may find it an advantage to dip these in varnish diluted with white spirit, to stop the ears dropping.

EASTER BASKET
The basic basket shape is made from cut lengths of straw and is filled with pressed pansies, violets, heather, marigold and cowslips.

FLY HOME SOON
A clever use of dried leaves. Let the leaves you select suggest an image to you. This design is made up of maple, ash and beech leaves.

HOMECOMING
This little bird, shaped from cut leaves, has built his nest with moss, twigs and feathers found in local woodland.

CAMEO
A classic dried flower arrangement created with a selection of wild flowers found in the hedgerow.

BUTTONS, BITS AND BOBS

Buttons, both old and new, come in a wonderful variety of shapes and colours and are the perfect decoration for greeting cards. Always take care to cut buttons off discarded clothing and keep them safely. A pasta jar full of buttons is decorative in its own right, so you have no excuse for throwing them out.

Short lengths of bead trim and lace can also be put to good use together with feathers and ribbons, which are also pretty incorporated in flower arrangements.

I have used black feathers in my Pow Wow card but, once you have traced and cut out the template on p.89, you can decorate the Indian headdress as simply or ornately as you choose.

You can even make cards from dried lentils and pasta, although spaghetti does tend to snap rather easily. I think the golden rule should be that you do not buy in any extra items but make imaginative use of things you find lying about.

There are many small gifts you may wish to send your friends: pot-pourri sachets, packets of garden seeds, children's novelties etc. These could be built into your card. When you take the trouble to frame little gifts in this way it suggests that a good deal of thought and caring went into them.

BUTTON UP!
A selection of buttons stitched on to shirting cotton for the man in your life.

CARD FOR A HAS-BEAN!
. . . Or a vegetarian's diamond wedding. Or maybe simply an invitation to dinner. This one is made from glueing braid to your card in a diamond and cross pattern and filling the diamonds with split pea and lentil flowers.

A CARD FOR THE ROMANTIC SOFTIE IN YOUR LIFE
It doesn't have to be Valentine's Day to tell someone you love them.

'YOU'LL NEVER GO TO SEED'
Packets of seeds can be so pretty they can be mounted and sent as they are. Write your message on the front above the flowers.

COME TO A POW-WOW
This card is cut in one piece with an extended arm that folds back and conceals your message. Draw in a face and decorate with felt-tipped pens, feathers and beads.

BUTTON BOUQUET
A pretty arrangement of old and new buttons on cream embroidery fabric. Suitable for any occasion.

GETTING THE MESSAGE

Having gone to the trouble of making your card, you do not want to spoil it by writing 'Happy Birthday' or whatever on the front in illegible, scrawly hand-writing.

I believe that the real message – that is, whatever you put on the inside – should be written personally. For the outside, however, there are various resources to help you produce a well-presented caption:

1. If you intend to make Christmas or birthday cards on a regular basis you should consider investing in rubber stamps. Interesting stamps are becoming widely available and if you purchase those that cover your basic message, you can select ink colours to match your design and produce some very professional-looking cards.

2. If you have a friend with a typewriter or word processor, why not bribe them into producing a page of general messages for you in interesting typefaces? Keep your master sheets and photocopy several sheets so that you can cut them out and glue them in your cards when required. Alternatively, you could cut out and mount messages from pre-printed cards that you have received in the past, glue them all on to one sheet and photocopy them for re-use.

3. If you want to attempt a caption yourself but do not feel that your handwriting is neat enough, practise on graph paper and, when you are happy with the results, trace your message on to the card.

4. Dry transfer lettering (Letraset) is by far the most professional, but it is fiddly to use and quite expensive. It does, however, allow you to select from no end of typefaces and you might consider it worthwhile spending some time using this method to create master copies of messages for use in all your projects. To allow for errors, it would be wise not to attempt to transfer this lettering directly on to your card, but to create the message on a sheet of paper which can then be glued in. In some instances this may help give a better finish; when, for example, a fabric design has required you to fold and glue fabric back to the inside of your card, you can now cover the waste with a sheet of message. The secret of successful dry transferring is alignment, so if you wish to have a go, give yourself plenty of time and a clear workspace.

5. Rulers which contain pre-cut stencils for lettering are available at most art shops. This method of message-writing gives you only one simple style to work with and you must still be careful with your lining-up. Despite these drawbacks you will probably find this method useful for a number of projects.

6. As a last resort, or to arm yourself with yet another useful skill, you might like to teach yourself the basics of calligraphy. You can obtain pen and nib sets very cheaply and there are numerous books on the subject, so why not have a go.

A JEWEL OF A CARD
You may not be able to afford the crown jewels but you can make this card for the treasure in your life.

OCCASIONS AND IDEAS

You shouldn't really need an excuse to send someone a card other than simply wanting to say 'greetings'. However, I list below a calendar of occasions together with suggestions for appropriate themes to base your images on.

HOLIDAYS AND FESTIVALS

JANUARY

1 January: New Year's Day (Hogmanay). A day of great celebration in Scotland.
Kilts, sporrans, tartan, whisky, Father Time, Auld Lang Syne, haggis, thistles. First-footing: bread, salt, coal or kindling.

6 January: Epiphany. Visit of the Wise Men to the baby Jesus. In Spain and Italy presents are exchanged at Epiphany instead of Christmas and the Magi bring the gifts to the children.
Wise men. Gold, frankincense and myrrh.

25 January: Burns' Night. Another Scottish holiday celebrating the birth of the poet Robert Burns.
As 1 January plus Burns' poetry.

Between 21 January and 20 February: Chinese New Year. First full moon in February. The date changes every year depending on the lunar calendar.
The animal of the year: rat, ox, tiger, rabbit, dragon, snake, horse, goat, monkey, rooster, dog, pig – check which one is appropriate to the new year (see p.81). The Lion Dance, the colour red, drums and cymbals, fireworks and lanterns. 'Red packets' containing money. Kung Hei Fat Choy – Happy New Year.

26 January: Australia Day.
Kangaroos, koalas, wallabies, boomerangs, hats with corks dangling from them, the song 'Waltzing Matilda', eucalyptus trees.

FEBRUARY

Between 3 February and 9 March: Shrove Tuesday or Mardi Gras ('fat Tuesday'). In many European countries this is the last day of carnival, before the beginning of Lent, and a great excuse for a party.
Pancakes (recipes for), carnival paraphernalia, masks.

6 February: New Zealand Day or Waitangi.
'Land of the Long White Cloud'–sheep, anything woolly, kiwis.

14 February: St Valentine's Day.
Hearts, flowers, lace, satin, poems, cupids.

Late February–early March: Holi. Hindu festival celebrating the end of winter and the beginning of spring. A time for fun, tricks and dancing, when people throw coloured water at each other.
Birds, flowers, trees, grain and coconuts, maypoles, sugar cones.

MARCH

1 March: St David's Day. Feast day of the patron saint of Wales.
Daffodils, Welsh costume, recipes for Welsh cakes, rugby, love spoons, red dragons, leeks.

3 March: Dolls Festival (Japan). Also known as the Girls Festival or the Peach Blossom Festival.
Dolls, peach blossom.

4 March–7 April (4th Sunday in Lent): Mothering Sunday.
Spring flowers, mother's favourite things, perfumed sachets, breakfast in bed, medals, certificates of merit, poems.

17 March: St Patrick's Day. Feast day of the patron saint of Ireland.
Shamrocks, harps, leprechauns, round towers, Celtic crosses, pots of gold, jigs, recipe for potato cakes, anything green.

22 March–24 April: Easter. Celebration of the resurrection of Jesus from the dead (falls on the Sunday after the first full moon following 21 March).
Eggs, baskets, bunnies, chicks, spring flowers, ducklings, bonnets, recipe for Simnel cake.

27 March–24 April: Passover.
Angels, all traditions relating to Seder night, e.g. matzos, parting of the Red Sea, sweet and bitter herbs etc., recipes.

APRIL

1 April: All Fool's Day.
Jesters, jokers, joke cards, pop-ups, cards containing squeakers, spot the deliberate mistake.

23 April: St George's Day. Feast day of the patron saint of England.
Dragons, maidens in distress, castles, English rose, Tudor rose, knights in armour, map of England, gestures and rhymes relating to gallantry, Union Jack flag.

April (date changes annually): Baisakhi. Celebration of the great Sikh leader Gobind Rai's creation of the Khalsa, to whom he gave five things each beginning with a 'K' in Punjab.
Swords, bracelets, combs, lions.

Last Saturday in April: Arbor Day (US).
Tree planting, anything connected with trees or leaves.

MAY

1 May: May Day or Labour Day. The beginning of the Celtic summer.
Maypole, ribbons, wild flowers, apple blossom, birch twigs, lily of the valley (France).

2 or 3 May: Rice Planting Festival (Japan). The start of the working year.
Rice and its implements, bamboo poles, sake, traditional designs.

2nd Sunday in May: Mother's Day (US and Canada). See above.

May or June (on the full moon day of the month Visakha): Vesak. Most important Buddhist festival celebrating the life of Buddha. Captured birds, fish or turtles are released to show the love and compassion of Buddha. Hospitality and generosity are shown to the monks.
Images of Buddha, incense sticks, rice, coins, candles and flowers (lotus blossom), Bodhi trees.

JUNE

June: Maori New Year (New Zealand).
Song and dance, spring-cleaning ceremonies.

3rd Sunday in June: Father's Day.
Anything relating to dad's hobbies, idiosyncrasies, favourite meals, job etc.

Midsummer (the 5th day of the 5th month in the Chinese lunar calendar): Chinese Dragon Boat festival.
Dragons, masks, streamers, Chinese flowers, current year symbol (see p.81), papercrafts, rice, dragon shaped boats.

JULY

1 July: Canada Day.
Canadian flag, maple leaves, Mounties, beavers.

4 July: Independence Day (US).
American flag, fireworks, pop-ups of celebrations, Liberty Bell, people waving flags, Statue of Liberty, cheerleaders, all things American.

14 July: Bastille Day (France).
Blue, white and red rosettes, recipe for frogs' legs, Eiffel Tower, tricoteuses (ladies knitting).

July – August: Eil ul-Adha, Festival of Sacrifice (Muslim). Falls in the 12th month of the Islamic year at the end of the Hajj. Eid cards and gifts are given.
Islamic patterns.

AUGUST

1 August: Lammas or Lughnasa. Celtic Harvest Festival.
Corn, milk, fruit and fish.

Meelad ul-Nabi. Celebration of the birth of the Prophet Muhammad. The date falls twelve days earlier each year.
A beautiful calligraphic copy of the Prophet's name, or anything provided it isn't perfect, since nature itself is imperfect and in Islam man may not be seen to place himself above nature.

SEPTEMBER

9 September: Chrysanthemum Festival (Japan). A late summer festival. Autumn, harvest, joviality, wealth, longevity and happiness.
Flowers (especially chrysanthemums) and fruits.

Late September – early October: Rosh Hashanah. Jewish New Year.
Apples, honey, Hebrew lettering (see Working with Needles for correct letters) in various media.

2nd Sunday in September: Grandparent's Day.
Anything relating to their hobbies, photos or photocopies incorporating grandchildren, needlework cards with special messages, hearts, flowers.

Any date in September: Harvest Festival or Harvest Home.
Mice, corn, fruit, vegetables especially marrows, seeds, recipes, scenes of interiors, houses, comfort, home.

29 September: Michaelmas.
Celtic symbols, dragons, harvest.

OCTOBER

31 October: Hallowe'en.
Witches, pumpkins, bats, lanterns.

October–November: Diwali, Hindu festival of lights. The start of the new year, closing the books, the triumph of Rama and Sita, with the aid of the monkey god Hanuman, over the ten-headed demon king Ravana.
Candles, lamps, monkeys, little boats made of leaves or coconut shells, elaborate patterns, crows, cows and dogs.

NOVEMBER

5 November: Guy Fawkes Day.
Fireworks, guy, bonfires

4th Thursday of November (US) or 2nd Monday of October (Canada): Thanksgiving.
As for Harvest Festival plus turkeys, cranberries, nuts, berries.

11 November: Martinmas (France, Germany). Feast of St Martin, patron saint of the needy and homeless.
Knitted swatches/mini scarves, since traditionally St Martin gave a beggar his cloak. Also lanterns, for he was known to bring light into the life of the poor.

30 November: St Andrew's Day. Feast day of the patron saint of Scotland.
As for New Year's Day plus St Andrew's Cross (X-shaped).

DECEMBER

6 December: St Nicholas' Day (northern Europe).
Santa Claus, gifts, three golden balls, Black Peter and his birch twigs.

Early December: Chanukkah. Jewish Festival of Lights.
Seven-branched candelabra.

13 December: St Lucia's Day (Scandinavia).
Stars, candles, crowns and garlands.

25 December: Christmas Day.
Holly, ivy, mistletoe, reindeer, Santa Claus, robins, snow scenes, presents, stockings, turkeys, plum puddings, mince pies, Mary and Jesus, stables, three kings, stars, donkeys, angels, St Nicholas (Holland), sabots (France and Switzerland).

BIRTHDAYS:

ASTROLOGICAL SIGN	SYMBOL	LUCKY COLOUR	NUMBER	DAY	GEMSTONE	CHARACTERISTICS
Aries: March 20–April 19	Ram	Red	9	Tuesday	Diamond/Jasper	I am
Taurus: April 20–May 20	Bull	Blue/Mauve	6	Friday	Sapphire/Jade	I have
Gemini: May 21–June 20	Twins	Yellow	5	Wednesday	Emerald/Agate	I think
Cancer: June 21–July 21	Crab	Silver/White	2 & 7	Monday	Pearl/Moonstone	I feel
Leo: July 22–August 22	Lion	Gold	1	Sunday	Diamond/Ruby	I will
Virgo: August 23–Sept 22	Virgin	Navy/Autumn	5	Wednesday	Topaz/Peridot	I analyse
Libra: Sept 23–Oct 22	Scales	Turquoise	6	Friday	Beryl/Sapphire	I balance
Scorpio: Oct 23–Nov 21	Scorpion	Dark red	9	Tuesday	Opal	I desire
Sagittarius: Nov 22–Dec 20	Archer	Purple	3	Thursday	Topaz	I see
Capricorn: Dec 21–Jan 19	Goat	Brown/Black	8	Saturday	Sapphire/Turquoise	I use
Aquarius: Jan 20–Feb 17	Water Bearer	White/Green	4	Saturday	Aquamarine/Amber	I know
Pisces: Feb 18–March 19	Fish	Sea green/pastels	3 & 7	Thursday	Amethyst/Moonstone	I believe

If you have any friends with birthdays on a Sunday, send them this:

'Monday's child is fair of face,
Tuesday's child is full of grace,
Wednesday's child is full of woe,
Thursday's child has far to go,
Friday's child is loving and giving,
Saturday's child works hard for a living
But the child that's born on the Sabbath day
Is bonny and blithe and good and gay.' (Anon.)

18th BIRTHDAY:

Key to the door, champagne, Statue of Liberty, medal, photo of favourite rock band, hobby-related item.

BON VOYAGE:

Boats and trains and planes, sunshine, beaches, holiday paraphernalia, luggage labels, stamps, hot air balloon.

CHRISTENINGS/NEW ARRIVALS:

Cradles, storks, washing lines full of baby clothes (Germany), teddies, baby rabbits and ducklings, lace keepsakes, dummies, embroidered names, family trees, appropriate birthday newspaper cuttings mounted in a card, astrological symbol, year's animal (Chinese).

DIVORCE:

Congratulations on becoming single: Medal and Certificate for Freedom of the City, Personal Flag to declare State of Independence, crossed swords, 'Under New Management' badge, released jailbird.

ENGAGEMENT:

Flowers, intertwined names/initials, cards incorporating gemstones, silhouettes, his and her teddies, doves, animals, birds and bees.

GET WELL SOON:

Here is a little rhyme that might provide some food for thought:

'Sneeze on Monday, sneeze for danger,
Sneeze on Tuesday, kiss a stranger.
Sneeze on Wednesday, sneeze for a letter,
Sneeze on Thursday, something better.
Sneeze on Friday, sneeze for sorrow,
Sneeze on Saturday, see your sweetheart tomorrow.'

Also: patchwork quilts, pressed flowers/bookmarks, old herbal recipes/remedies, perfumed cards relating to aromatherapy. (Either include a small pot-pourri sachet or sprinkle a drop of essential oil on the inside of your card. This is particularly suitable for cards that contain a padded image, but remember to drop the essential oil on the padding inside the motif to prevent staining.)

GOOD LUCK (driving test, examinations, job interview, new job etc.):

Black cats, horseshoes, four-leaf clovers, the number 7, white heather.

NEW HOME:

Houses, cottages, snails, tortoises, castles, palaces, skyscrapers, bird's nest, lion's den, cave, beehive, fox's lair.

PARTY INVITATIONS:

Champagne, glasses, streamers, cancan girls, musical notes, balloons.

RETIREMENT:

Certificate proclaiming a new lease on life, seed packets, symbols based on hobbies, gold cup.

WEDDING:

Bows, bells, something old, new, borrowed, blue, garters, floral posies, silver horseshoes, slippers, confetti.

WEDDING ANNIVERSARIES:

1st	paper	13th	lace
2nd	cotton	14th	ivory
3rd	leather	15th	crystal
4th	fruit and flowers	20th	china
5th	wood	25th	silver
6th	sugar and cakes	30th	pearl
7th	wool	35th	coral
8th	salt	40th	ruby
9th	copper	45th	sapphire
10th	tin	50th	gold
11th	steel	55th	emerald
12th	silk and fine linen	60th	diamond

OTHER OCCASIONS:

Congratulations:
On pregnancy, on acquiring a new dog/cat, on adopting a baby, on giving up smoking, on losing weight, on paying back your overdraft, on settling your mortgage.

Messages:
I miss you. I'm sorry. Thank you. Belated Birthdays. Ring Me. Let's Have Lunch. Get Lost.

YEARS CORRESPONDING TO THE CHINESE SIGNS

THE RAT	THE OX	THE TIGER
31.1.1900/18.2.1901	19.2.1901/ 7.2.1902	8.2.1902/28.1.1903
18.2.1912/ 5.2.1913	6.2.1913/25.1.1914	26.1.1914/13.2.1915
5.2.1924/24.1.1925	25.1.1925/12.2.1926	13.2.1926/ 1.2.1927
24.1.1936/10.2.1937	11.2.1937/30.1.1938	31.1.1938/18.2.1939
10.2.1948/28.1.1949	29.1.1949/16.2.1950	17.2.1950/ 5.2.1951
28.1.1960/14.2.1961	15.2.1961/ 4.2.1962	5.2.1962/24.1.1963
15.2.1972/ 2.2.1973	3.2.1973/22.1.1974	23.1.1974/10.2.1975
2.2.1984/19.2.1985	20.2.1985/ 8.2.1986	9.2.1986/28.1.1987
19.2.1996/ 6.2.1997	7.2.1997/21.1.1998	28.1.1998/15.2.1999

THE RABBIT	THE DRAGON	THE SNAKE
29.1.1903/15.2.1904	16.2.1904/ 3.2.1905	4.2.1905/24.1.1906
14.2.1915/ 2.2.1916	3.2.1916/22.1.1917	23.1.1917/10.2.1918
2.2.1927/22.1.1928	23.1.1928/ 9.2.1929	10.2.1929/29.1.1930
19.2.1939/ 7.2.1940	8.2.1940/26.1.1941	27.1.1941/14.2.1942
6.2.1951/26.1.1952	27.1.1952/13.2.1953	14.2.1953/ 2.2.1954
25.1.1963/12.2.1964	13.2.1964/ 1.2.1965	2.2.1965/20.1.1966
11.2.1975/30.1.1976	31.1.1976/17.2.1977	18.2.1977/ 6.2.1978
29.1.1987/16.2.1988	17.2.1988/ 5.2.1989	6.2.1989/26.1.1990
16.2.1999/ 4.2.2000	5.2.2000/23.1.2001	24.1.2001/11.2.2002

THE HORSE	THE GOAT	THE MONKEY
25.1.1906/12.2.1907	13.2.1907/ 1.2.1908	2.2.1908/21.1.1909
11.2.1918/31.1.1919	1.2.1919/19.2.1920	20.2.1920/ 7.2.1921
30.1.1930/16.2.1931	17.2.1931/ 5.2.1932	6.2.1932/25.1.1933
15.2.1942/ 4.2.1943	5.2.1943/24.1.1944	25.1.1944/12.2.1945
3.2.1954/23.1.1955	24.1.1955/11.2.1956	12.2.1956/30.1.1957
21.1.1966/ 8.2.1967	9.2.1967/28.1.1968	29.1.1968/16.2.1969
7.2.1978/27.1.1979	28.1.1979/15.2.1980	16.2.1980/ 4.2.1981
27.1.1990/14.2.1991	15.2.1991/ 3.2.1992	4.2.1992/22.1.1993
12.2.2002/31.1.2003	1.2.2003/21.1.2004	22.1.2004/ 8.2.2005

THE ROOSTER	THE DOG	THE PIG
22.1.1909/ 9.2.1910	10.2.1910/29.1.1911	30.1.1911/17.2.1912
8.2.1921/27.1.1922	28.1.1922/15.2.1923	16.2.1923/ 4.2.1924
26.1.1933/13.2.1934	14.2.1934/ 3.2.1935	4.2.1935/23.1.1936
13.2.1945/ 1.2.1946	2.2.1946/21.1.1947	22.1.1947/ 9.2.1948
31.1.1957/15.2.1958	16.2.1958/ 7.2.1959	8.2.1959/27.1.1960
17.2.1969/ 5.2.1970	6.2.1970/26.1.1971	27.1.1971/14.2.1972
5.2.1981/24.1.1982	25.1.1982/12.2.1983	13.2.1983/ 1.2.1984
23.1.1993/ 9.2.1994	10.2.1994/30.1.1995	31.1.1995/18.2.1996
9.2.2005/28.1.2006	29.1.2006/17.2.2007	18.2.2007/6.2.2008

The dates indicated specify the *first* and the *last* day of the year of the sign.

SUNFLOWER

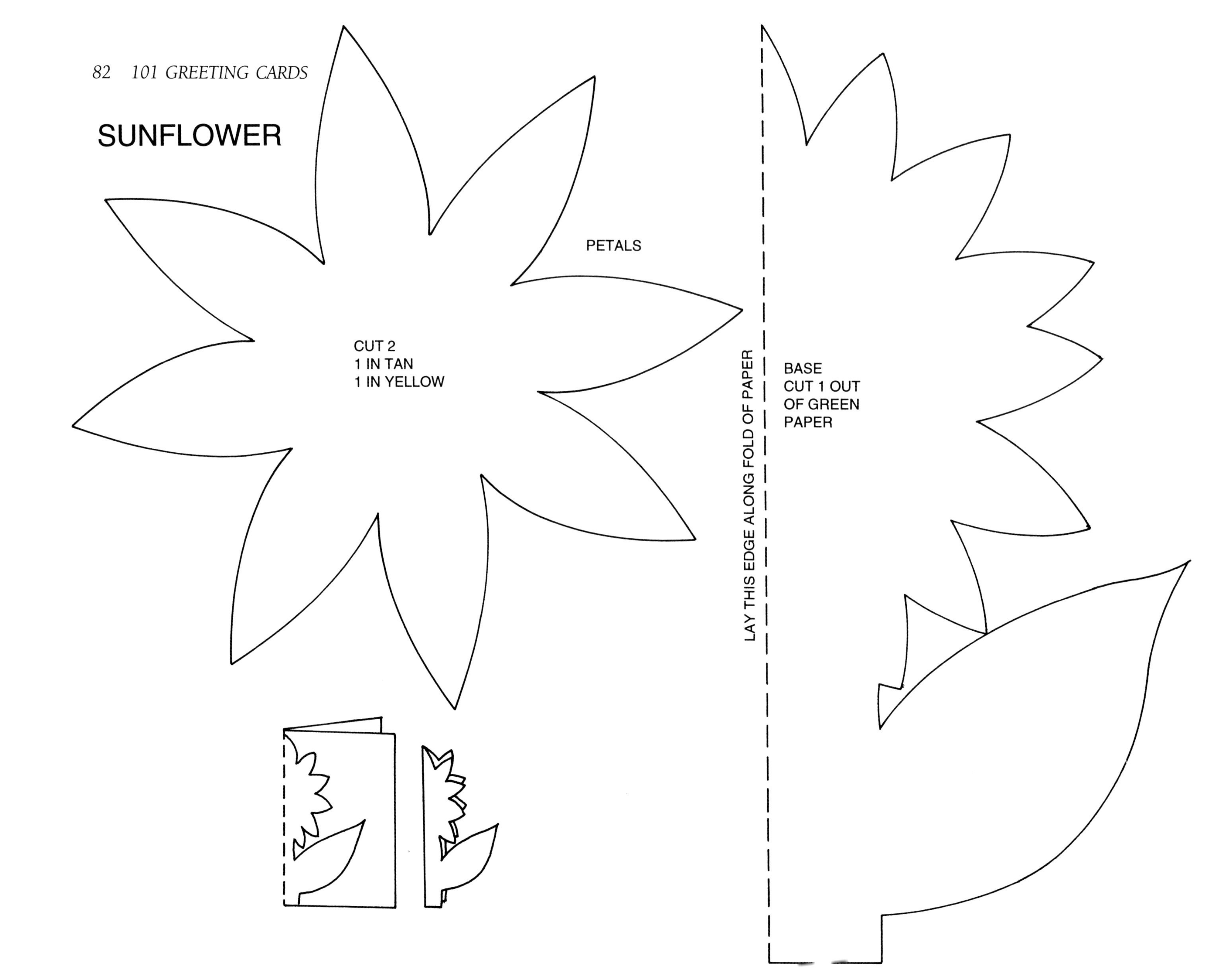
PETALS
CUT 2
1 IN TAN
1 IN YELLOW
LAY THIS EDGE ALONG FOLD OF PAPER
BASE
CUT 1 OUT
OF GREEN
PAPER

MR CRAB

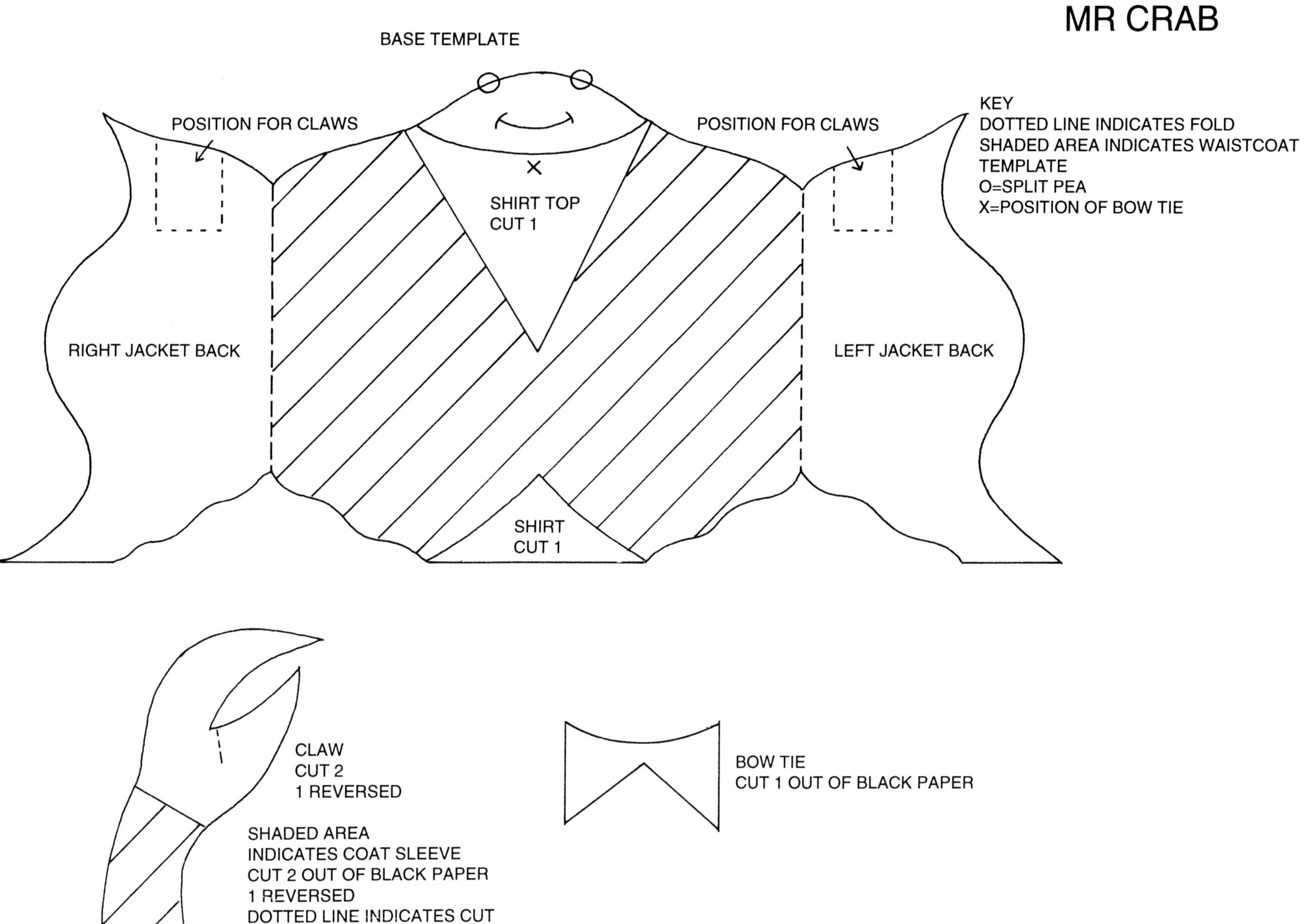
BASE TEMPLATE
POSITION FOR CLAWS
POSITION FOR CLAWS
KEY
DOTTED LINE INDICATES FOLD
SHADED AREA INDICATES WAISTCOAT TEMPLATE
O=SPLIT PEA
X=POSITION OF BOW TIE
SHIRT TOP
CUT 1
RIGHT JACKET BACK
LEFT JACKET BACK
SHIRT
CUT 1
CLAW
CUT 2
1 REVERSED
SHADED AREA
INDICATES COAT SLEEVE
CUT 2 OUT OF BLACK PAPER
1 REVERSED
DOTTED LINE INDICATES CUT
BOW TIE
CUT 1 OUT OF BLACK PAPER

1 TODAY

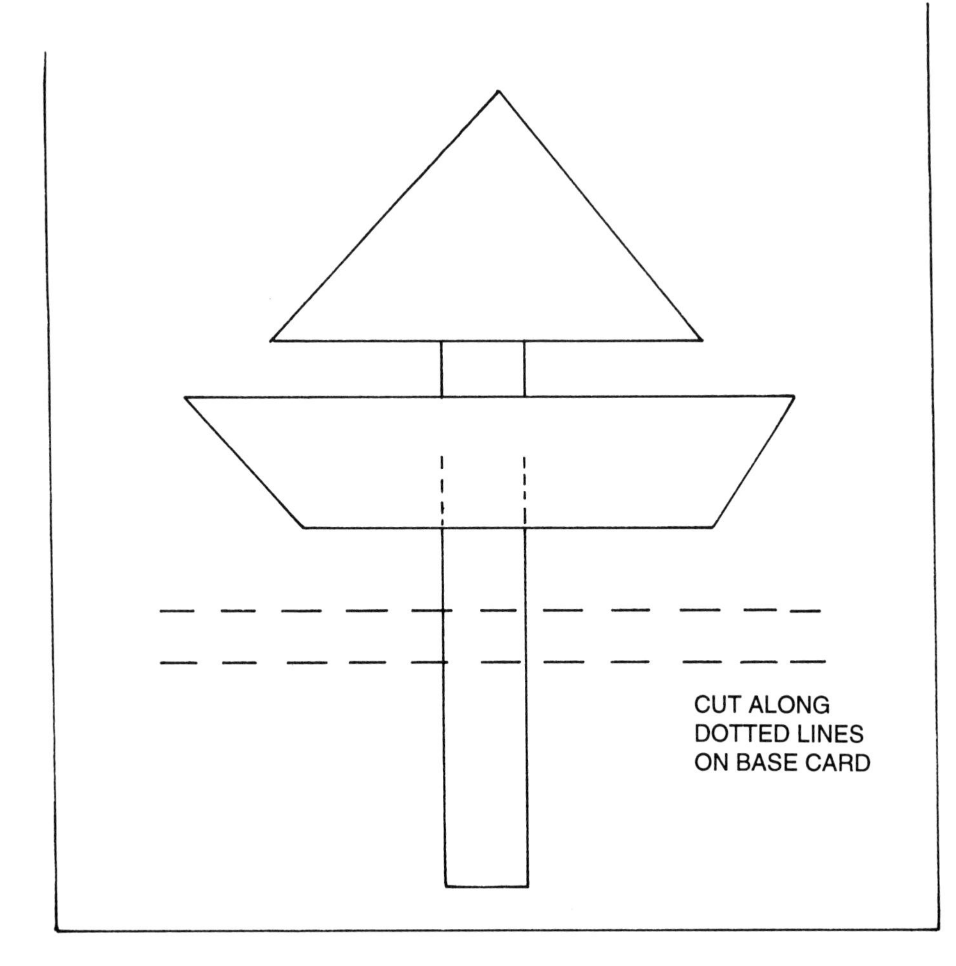

KEEP
SMILING
SUNSHINE

1 TODAY WAVE

5cm
1.5cm
2cm

HEAD
CUT 1 TEMPLATE

WISE OLD OWL

2

1

1

3

WING TEMPLATE
CUT 2

LAY AGAINST FOLD

MAIN TEMPLATE

TUMMY FEATHERS
CUT 17

WING FEATHERS
CUT 40

GLUE ENDS OF STRIPS
TO BACK LEAVING
OPENING FOR EYE FLAG

HOLE

HOLE

BASE TEMPLATE

CAT WITH NINE LIVES

EYE TEMPLATE

CUT 1

LAY ON FOLD OF CARD

YOU SNEAKY SO AND SO

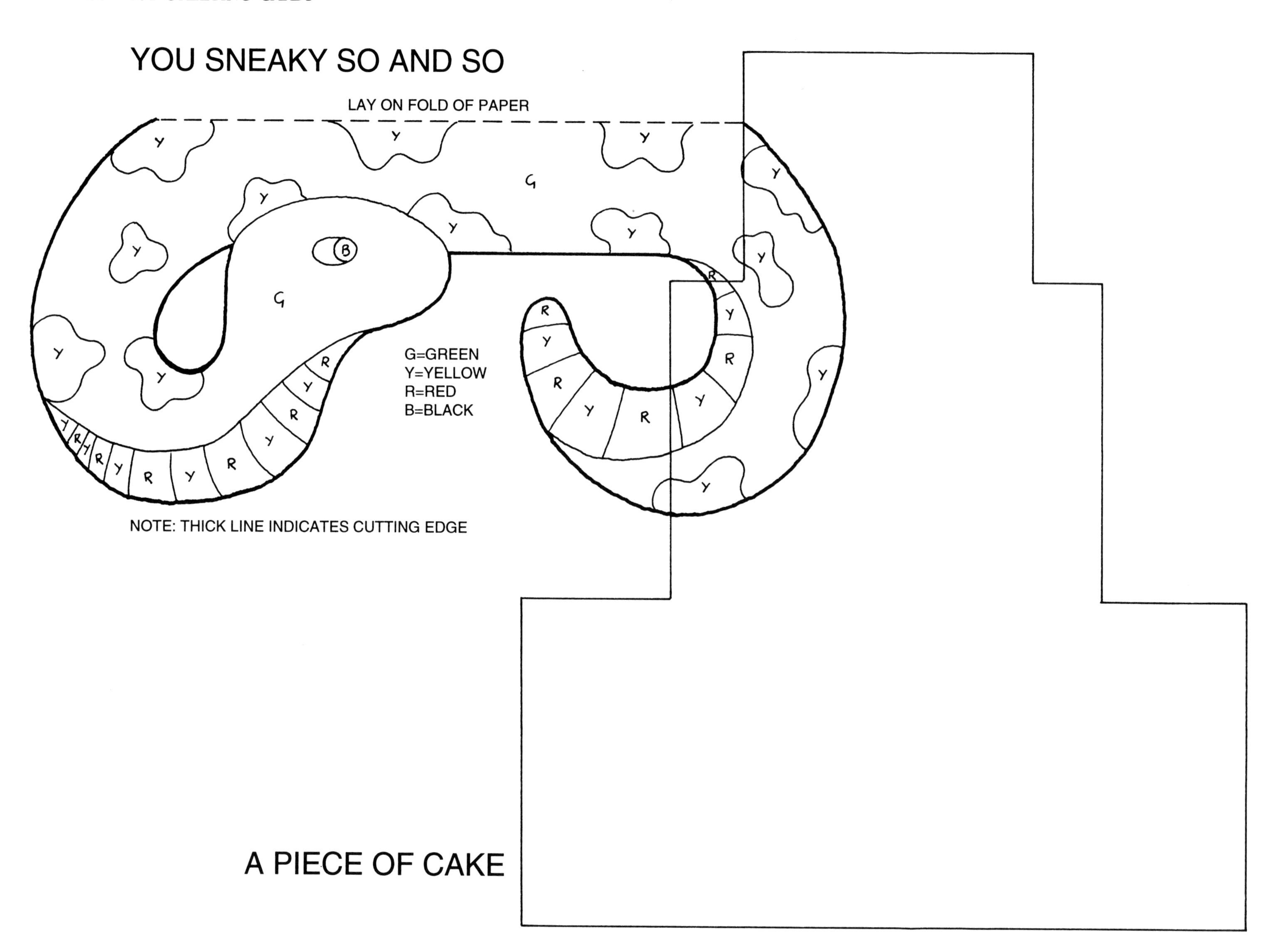

A PIECE OF CAKE

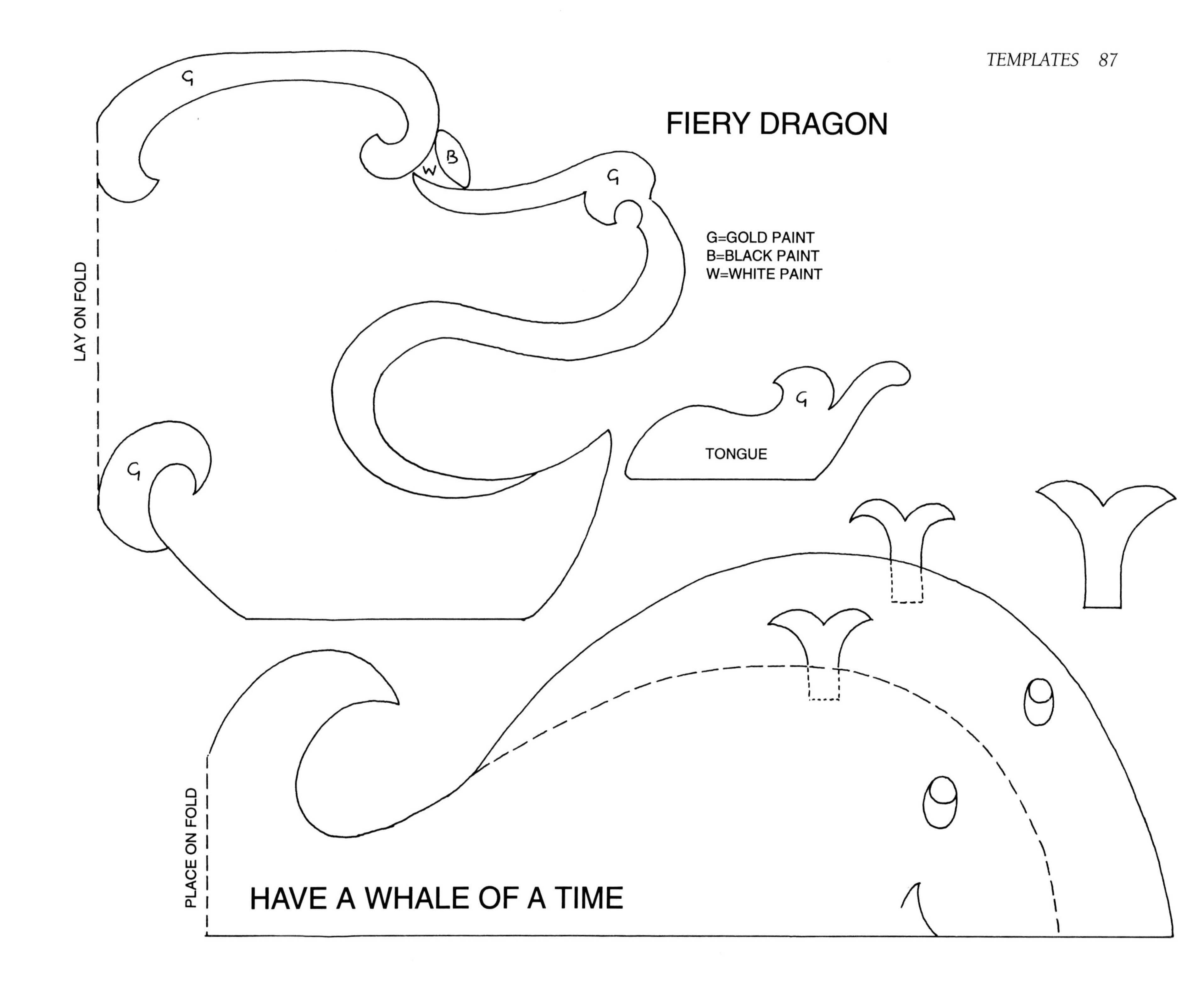
FIERY DRAGON
G=GOLD PAINT
B=BLACK PAINT
W=WHITE PAINT
G
G
G
G
W
B
LAY ON FOLD
TONGUE
HAVE A WHALE OF A TIME
PLACE ON FOLD

TEMPLATES

Cards can be any shape or size, although you must obviously consider the means of delivery. Many of the basic cards in this book are oblong in shape, measuring 16 cm x 11.5 cm. The following window templates are actual size and can be traced on to your basic card and cut out as required.

For decorative cards, it is a good idea to work on a three-fold principle, i.e. the card is divided horizontally into three equal-sized oblongs with the template cut from the middle panel. The oblong to the right as you look at it should be scored down the left edge with a knitting needle, ready for folding back, and the oblong on the left should be scored down the right edge for the same purpose. The right-hand oblong when folded back will hide your glueing etc. and make for a more substantial card.

OBLONG / SQUARE

HEART

OVAL

FOUR PANED WINDOW

WINDOW TEMPLATES